MORE PRAISE FOR
How to Save Democracy

"We have all heard certainly after January 6, 2021, that we cannot take democracy for granted. But what does that mean in practice? As Eli Merritt shows in this slim, powerful volume, it means enacting and defending a specific set of human values and ensuring that there is accountability whenever those values are attacked. By quoting today's world leaders on the importance of democracy, Merritt has performed an invaluable service: to hold the powerful to their word, while holding the rest of us, the people, responsible for protecting the best system of government yet devised."

Jesse Wegman, member of the *New York Times* editorial board and author of *Let the People Pick the President*

"This fine book brings together profound transnational insights on the promise of and perils to democracy. The universality of the quest for representative government is demonstrated in a compelling fashion. Of equal importance, this volume leaves no doubt about the practical foundations of a successful democracy. Democracy is indeed a project of humanity, and achieving it is hard work and needs structure and inspiration. Eli Merritt provides both in great surplus. A must-read for everyone in these times, but especially for anyone entering the political sphere!"

Nick Zeppos, chancellor emeritus
and distinguished professor of law and
political science at Vanderbilt University

"How to Save Democracy is a valuable educational resource not only for students K–12 but also for college students and adults of all ages. It speaks to me because it inspires hope and activism while also providing concrete strategies for safeguarding democracy from corruption. In this way, it is two-books-in-one: a collection of poetic quotations and simultaneously a how-to-save-democracy guide. Highly recommended also for parents, teachers, activists, journalists, and nonprofits."

Martha Ingram, former chairman of
the Vanderbilt Board of Trust

"The forces of authoritarianism, both at home and abroad, are staging a concerted assault on democracy, one of the most aggressive attacks on freedom that we have experienced since World War II. From the January 6 insurrection at the US Capitol to the brutal Russian invasion of Ukraine, the enemies of democracy have made their objectives plain. Americans and others around the world must join forces to protect democracy, and reading *How to Save Democracy* is a good place to start to fight back."

James Risen, Pulitzer Prize–winning author of *The Last Honest Man: The CIA, the FBI, the Mafia, and the Kennedys—and One Senator's Fight to Save Democracy*

"Women's rights and the protection of our democracies around the world are inextricably linked. Those seeking to debilitate democracies often start by depriving women of their basic rights. What is needed to sustain this incredibly important effort to stem the anti-democratic tide? The compilation of quotations in *How to Save Democracy* gives us answers, sustenance, and inspiration to help power through one of the darkest periods in our history. We must all have the discipline of hope and find inspiration in one another and in the democratic leaders of our time."

Andrea Dew Steele, founder of Emerge America

"As Jimmy Carter once said, 'We become not a melting pot but a beautiful mosaic. Different people, different beliefs, different yearnings, different hopes, different dreams.' These are the same ideals that suffuse *How to Save Democracy* and the ones we must return to in order to restore our magnificent democracy."

Jim Free, special assistant for congressional affairs to President Jimmy Carter (1977–1981)

"The struggle we witness today over the future of democracy and the need to defend it can seem complicated and daunting, but *How to Save Democracy* makes clear a unified message that is both simple and compelling. This remarkable compilation of thoughts from ninety-five world leaders demonstrates that democracy's defenders are widespread around the globe. These valuable pages should also inspire all Americans to positive civic action in our communities today."

Keel Hunt, *USA Today* network columnist and author of *Crossing the Aisle*

"Celebrated champion of democracy Lani Guinier once wrote: 'Democracy isn't something we inherit. It is not something we inhabit. It is not something we consume. It's something we actively build together.' This excellent collection of quotations will inspire our essential work to build strong and resilient twenty-first-century democracies where all people have a seat at the table."

Cynthia Richie Terrell, founder and director of RepresentWomen

"American political commentary tends toward the parochial, but in *How to Save Democracy* Merritt offers us a remarkable breadth of global perspectives that reminds us not only of the value of democracy but that complacency is the surest path to its loss."

Frederic C. Rich, author of *Christian Nation* and *Getting to Green*

"Demagogues and authoritarians are on the rise, and the number of democracies has declined each year for over a decade. Defenders of liberal democracy of every political persuasion must bury their differences and unite around the core strategies set out in *How to Save Democracy*."

Richard A. Wilson, board of trustees professor, University of Connecticut School of Law

"This book contains powerful wisdom to guide citizens and business leaders, immigrants who struggle to find a new home, and veterans who have bled for freedom on the necessity of fighting for our democracy every day. As Guy Parmelin, president of Switzerland, said in the 'Core Values' section, 'Democracy is never achieved. It is a work in constant progress.'"

Erik Wohlgemuth, CEO of Future 500

"Democracy is hard work, as President Joe Biden noted, but these inspiring quotations from ninety-five world leaders chosen by Eli Merritt encourage us all to do the hard work of safeguarding and sustaining this magnificent and free form of government."

Gray Sasser, executive director of the Vanderbilt Project on Unity and American Democracy

"The US Constitution's preamble begins with 'We the People,' and Americans are called to protect, nurture and sustain our republic. But democracy in America is imperiled by apathy, opportunism, and the dehumanization of our fellow citizens. As this timely book reminds us, page after page, defending democracy is not someone else's job. It is the everyday duty of every citizen who values liberty, fairness, and good will toward their neighbors. This is what will lead us to a more perfect union."

David Plazas, opinion and engagement director, *USA Today* Network Tennessee; and Champion, Civility Tennessee Campaign

"Eli Merritt's *How to Save Democracy* is a wonderful compendium of practical wisdom from a wide variety of leaders on the ideas and values we need to nurture and cherish in order to protect the world's democracies as we face the challenges to come."

Andrew Trees, author of *The Founding Fathers and the Politics of Character*

"*How to Save Democracy* is a powerful, sobering, and inspiring guide for safeguarding the free world we wish to live in. This book is an elegant distillation of the basic principles, problems, opportunities, dreams, and tools that can help fortify democracy. It shows us how to thrive and prosper with our rights and freedoms intact, and it outlines concrete strategies to accomplish just that."

Vanessa Burnett, founder of Shift the Country

"Sometimes it takes a crisis for us to realize what we value and why. At the end of the Cold War, democracy came to be taken for granted, seen as inevitable. Yet recent events reveal its fragility. This educational and inspirational volume collects compelling insights on the ideals and promise of democracy, and it also provides a practical guide for what we can do to protect it. Open *How to Save Democracy* to any page, and you will find captivating and concise practical wisdom, reminding us of the values that unite us in the face of increasing polarization."

Ted Fischer, Cornelius Vanderbilt professor of anthropology and author of *The Good Life*

"Reinhold Niebuhr said it best: 'Man's capacity for justice makes democracy possible, but man's inclination to injustice makes democracy necessary.' No one in any corner of the world is safe, even in the United States, from the would-be tyrants who want to aggrandize themselves by robbing you of your freedoms. Don't let them. Read *How to Save Democracy* and learn how to protect yourself, your family, and your democracy."

Congressman Jim Cooper, US House of Representatives (1983–1995, 2003–2023)

www.amplifypublishinggroup.com

How to Save Democracy: Advice and Inspiration from 95 World Leaders

The publisher assumes no responsibility for errors, inaccuracies, omissions, or any other inconsistencies herein. All the quotations contained in this book are derived from the speeches of world leaders at the first international Summit for Democracy, transcribed by the author.

For more information, please contact:
Amplify Publishing, an imprint of Amplify Publishing Group
620 Herndon Parkway, Suite 320
Herndon, VA 20170
info@amplifypublishing.com

ISBN-13: 979-8-9872952-2-9

Printed in the United States

More Advice and Inspiration from World Leaders

The quotations about democracy contained in this book are derived from the speeches of world leaders at the first international Summit for Democracy. Videos of the speeches are indexed on the US Department of State's "Summit for Democracy" web page.

A second Summit for Democracy is scheduled for late March of 2023. At its conclusion, I will gather more advice and inspiration from the leaders of the world's democracies into a second collection and make it available on my website (elimerritt.com).

The two overriding purposes of *How to Save Democracy* are education and inspiration to get involved. In this spirit RepresentUs and I encourage citizens everywhere to come together to rescue democracy from disinformation, demagoguery, corruption, authoritarianism, and violence. Active citizenship is not only the best way forward to build the free and ethical societies we wish to hand down to our children and grandchildren. It is the only way forward.

As President Volodymyr Zelensky of Ukraine said at the first summit, "By coming together, we will make this world freer, safer, and more democratic."

~Eli Merritt

Advice and Inspiration from
95 World Leaders

HOW

TO SAVE

DEMOCRACY

Edited and with an Introduction by
ELI MERRITT
Foreword by Joshua Graham Lynn

amplify
an imprint of Amplify Publishing Group

Contents

III. THE WAY FORWARD

Foreword

Joshua Graham Lynn

How to Save Democracy effortlessly captures the historic moment we find ourselves in today. With the rise of corruption, misinformation, and authoritarianism around the world, it serves as a necessary wake-up call that we can't take freedom for granted. The book also charts an inspiring pathway forward. Reading the words of leaders from all four hemispheres, you'll find hope that if we unite across political differences, we can move past this perilous moment. We can continue this beautiful yet imperfect American experiment that has given so much to so many, and we can continue to stand as a beacon of freedom to people everywhere.

As the leader of RepresentUs, a fiercely nonpartisan organization dedicated to eradicating the corruption corroding American democracy, I was immediately drawn to this book. At its core, our work is about making sure the American people not only have a voice in our government but the loudest voice. We strive to build an America where our government is truly responsive and accountable to the people. Since the founding of RepresentUs ten years ago, we've seen warning signs that our democracy is backsliding, yet also tremendous potential for progress.

Like many democracies, the United States is experiencing a crisis of confidence in government fueled by corruption. Our broken campaign finance and ethics laws mean that politicians spend more time fundraising for themselves and their political party than they do working for the people they're elected to serve. With partisan gerrymandering, politicians and parties effectively rig their own elections and ensure they hold on to power. And even though nearly half of Americans are not registered with either major party and want better choices, we're often stuck with a binary vote between two candidates in a game of selecting the "lesser of two evils."

The result? According to a Princeton University study, it all adds up to the average American having "near-zero impact on public policy." No wonder Americans across the political spectrum, voters and nonvoters alike, feel powerless. We desperately need to change things.

And we can. Throughout American history, issues facing seemingly insurmountable odds have clenched victory from the jaws of defeat by following a disciplined, strategic approach. For us and our movement, this approach includes:

1. **Putting country over party**. We know voters across the political spectrum want to eliminate corruption and want politicians to be accountable to the people,

not special interests. We garner that broad support to break down political barriers, unite unlikely allies, and galvanize a truly cross-partisan movement to make lasting change.

2. **Building a movement that reaches beyond politics and helps reshape culture**. By uniting artists; academics; community, faith, and political leaders; businesses; and more, we create and foster a collective voice calling for change. We empower this movement with a sophisticated political strategy, world-class media and communications, and find and elevate natural leaders.

3. **Winning transformative new laws in the states to build momentum to national victory**. From marriage equality to Prohibition, women's suffrage to interracial marriage, our history is filled with examples of winning movements that leveraged state-based reforms to build power and set the bar for change. Like each of these movements, we're not only building momentum; we're creating tangible change. We're cleaning up state governments and rebuilding the people's power with every victory.

Over the last decade, RepresentUs and the anti-corruption movement have secured more than 170 local and state wins that give political power back to the voters. Each win shows that progress is possible and ushers in real change. When Alaska adopted nonpartisan primaries and Ranked Choice Voting, the 50 percent of registered independents in Alaska got to participate in primaries for the first time in thirty years—and the people of Alaska got better choices on the very next ballot. When Colorado implemented independent redistricting commissions, the entire face of state government changed, and with it the state itself. This is the power of what we can do when we dedicate ourselves to fighting corruption and protecting and strengthening our democracy.

The Summit for Democracy and the many quotations from world leaders in *How to Save Democracy* give me a tremendous sense of hope. Their inspiring words serve as important reminders that as imperfect as democracy is, it's our best chance to make progress, promote freedom, and continue advancing human rights around the world. And while democracies vary, they all strive to give ultimate power to the people—where it belongs.

At the end of the day, *How to Save Democracy* makes one thing clear: Despite the relentless attacks, and despite all its vulnerabilities, democracy is the best leadership structure that humanity knows. The leaders at the summit affirmed their commitment to democracy. The question is: Will we, the people, support them in protecting and strengthening it—and make sure always to hold them accountable? For the sake of future generations, I hope we will.

Introduction

Eli Merritt

I began *How to Save Democracy* during a period of grief in my life. My father, eighty-five years old, was dying of cancer. During the same month, I joined other Americans in mournful commemoration of the first anniversary of the January 6 insurrection. That historic day in 2021 represents a different sort of cancer in our lives—a cancer of demagoguery, corruption, and authoritarianism.

These events, however, coincided with the first international Summit for Democracy, where more than one hundred world leaders gathered virtually to inspire citizens to embrace hope and courage in the fight for ethical constitutional government. Spearheaded by President Joe Biden of the United States, the summit's mission was to unite democracies to the common purposes of beating back corruption, countering authoritarianism, and promoting respect for human rights. In his opening remarks, Biden notably warned against complacency in the face of a global tide of political leaders who seek to deceive, divide, and oppress. Arguing that a global recession of democracy is "the defining challenge of our time," he asked, "Will we allow the backward slide of rights and democracy to continue unchecked?"*

The solution, Biden said, is unity. "As a global community for democracy," he urged, "we have to stand up for the values that unite us. We have to stand for justice and the rule of law, for free speech, free assembly, a free press, freedom of religion, for all the inherent human rights of every individual."

I watched Biden's speech, and a hundred others, as a means of answering a keen personal question: What can I do to help protect democracy from further decline? The speakers laid out plenty of concrete solutions. Vastly more impactful, though, they conveyed passionate determination, something that lightened my burden and lifted my spirits.

"We must never forget that democracy is not simply a monolithic institutional construct," Mia Amor Mottley, prime minister of Barbados, said. "It is about people. And this is why we must commit always to seeing each other, to hearing each other, and to caring for each other. If we can do this, then we can give breath to democracy each and every day."†

---

* Remarks By President Biden at the Summit for Democracy Opening Session, December 9, 2021 (https://www.whitehouse.gov/briefing-room/speeches-remarks/2021/12/09/remarks-by-president-biden-at-the-summit-for-democracy-opening-session/).

† Prime Minister Mia Amor Mottley, Official Intervention, Summit for Democracy. All the quotations in this book are derived from the video links featured on the US Department of State's Official Interventions page (https://www.state.gov/official-interventions-the-summit-for-democracy/). Rarely, transcriptions of the official interventions are available online in print format.

Guy Parmelin, former president of Switzerland, put it this way: "Democracy, as government of the people, by the people, and for the people, has been a revolution in the history of mankind." Philip J. Pierre, prime minister of Saint Lucia, called democracy "our cherished way of life, which cannot be replaced by any other system of governance." He continued, saying that democracy "understands the natural inclination of people, irrespective of race, class, creed, or religion, to be free to live in peace, love, and dignity." Robert Abela, prime minister of Malta, called this free form of government "the greatest gift" that can be bestowed upon humankind.

Heartened and emboldened by words like these, I began to take notes and in the ensuing months gathered them into this volume for easy reading and reference. *How to Save Democracy* is a book for people of all ages and nationalities, but my greatest hope is that parents and teachers will hand it down to children and young adults because the challenges before them in the next half century will likely equal, if not exceed, our own.

Divided into three sections—"Virtues of Democracy," "Challenges and Threats," and "The Way Forward"—the book offers not only diverse perspectives on democracy but also abundant practical advice on how to strengthen free government to meet the challenges of the twenty-first century. *How to Save Democracy*, a collaboration with the nonprofit RepresentUs, one of the leading organizations in America fighting to protect and strengthen our democracy, is a powerful educational tool that teaches citizens six key principles of democratic success:

1. **Get involved**. Democracy, the best system of government ever conceived by the human mind, guarantees citizens human rights, peace, security, and opportunity. But maintaining democracy against the forces of demagoguery, corruption, and authoritarianism requires constant vigilance and effort. We must never take democracy for granted, and "We the People" must get involved. We must struggle for democracy every day in order to ensure that our children and grandchildren enjoy the same freedoms and rights in the future that we do today.

2. **Hold leaders accountable**. Democracy is the people's government. It is not a government of, by, and for the few, the rich, the corrupt, and the power hungry. The strength and legitimacy of democracy derives from active citizens who every day hold leaders of government, media, business, and education to high ethical and constitutional standards. Holding leaders accountable is a duty of those who live in a democracy. Citizens must relentlessly demand constitutionalism, justice, equality, the rule of law, and ethical leadership in order for democracy to survive.

3. **Demand free and fair elections.** The essence of democracy is the right of all citizens to make their voices heard through free, fair, and secure elections, and this promise can never be kept without sacred respect for the constitutions and courts that uphold

the rule of law. Here again the people must take action. They must demand constitutional free and fair elections, followed by the peaceful transfer of power from the losers of elections to the winners.

4. **Equality, inclusion, and diversity are cornerstones of democracy**. Elections are only free and fair if there is equal opportunity to vote, irrespective of race, religion, gender, sexuality, or economic status. Democracy is anchored in socially inclusive political and economic strategies, reflecting the will of the people. Diversity and inclusion are engines of creativity and critical thinking that bring about innovative solutions to new problems and threats, always driving democracies forward to new frontiers of equality and progress.

5. **Free and independent news media must pursue the truth**. News media is the means by which the public makes informed judgments and holds governments to account. Journalists enjoy freedom of the press, but they are also charged with the duty to pursue the truth relentlessly and to serve as watchdogs of democracy. Freedom of speech and freedom of the press are inviolable constitutional rights that come with great responsibility. The people must vigilantly oversee all forms of media in a democratic society, combatting demagoguery and falsehoods, demanding ethical behavior that adheres to democratic values of honesty, integrity, independence, accuracy, professionalism, and respect for all the citizens of a nation.

6. **Citizens, and nations, must unite to defend democracy.** Vigilant citizens are the most important watchdogs of all in the unceasing fight for ethical constitutional government. But to enjoy maximal power and success, they must unite. They must unite to prevent nations from sliding into demagoguery and authoritarianism. Citizens must organize, protest, write, sing, and dance as means to achieve constitutional protections for their rights and freedoms. Democratic nations, too, must unite globally to advance human rights and constitutionalism. In the digital era, collaboration and cooperation among democracies is the only pathway toward a more peaceful, prosperous, and democratic future.

The dual purposes of *How to Save Democracy* are education and inspiration to get involved and take action. This mission is similar to that of RepresentUs—which is to build a movement to create a government that is truly of, by, and for the people—and to *American Commonwealth*, my newsletter about the essential ethical values we must uphold in order to preserve our democratic institutions and freedoms. In the first section of the book, "Virtues of Democracy," leaders celebrate democracy as the best system of government in world history. In the words of Carlos Alvarado Quesada, president of Costa Rica, democracy is the only political order that guarantees "respect for dialogue, the promotion of tolerance, freedom of expression, and political pluralism. All of these values are necessary in order to achieve peace, progress, and well-being, the pillars upon which a true democratic society is built upon."

In his remarks, Alexander Schallenberg, former chancellor of Austria, reminded citizens that "democracy is not negotiable. Democracy is not a commodity. It is the only system capable of ensuring in a consistent manner our individual rights and freedoms, giving each of us the possibility to live up to the best of our potential."

The second section, "Challenges and Threats," spotlights corruption, disinformation, and authoritarianism as inveterate foes of democracy. "There is no bigger enemy to democracy than corruption," said Moon Jae-In, prime minister of South Korea. Keith Rowley of Trinidad and Tobago underscored that "a society free from corruption is a fundamental human right." Many of the leaders at the Summit for Democracy highlighted the novel threats posed by the exploitation of digital communications by malefactors. "Today most threats against democracy come from within—from elected leaders," Jonas Gahr Støre of Norway stated, "who act in breach of democratic principles, embrace corruption, and disregard human rights. The threat is often amplified by disinformation." Philip Davis, prime minister of the Bahamas, warned that "the historic roots of attack on democracy have been superseded. Tyranny can creep in not just via the bullet but via misinformation, via false advertising, the fake profile or vote—all of it fractures trust within our societies."

Salome Zourabichvili, president of Georgia, sounded a similar theme: "Democracies across the globe are now faced with hybrid warfare methods that include cyberattacks, disinformation, and targeted economic pressures and coercions. Democracies are also attacked from within. Polarization, fake news, and hate speech not only fuel internal divisions but also undermine public institutions and democratic processes, including trust in elections or in the media, two of the pillars of democracy."

Of course, it is demagogues, authoritarians, and their collaborators who debilitate and finally topple functioning democracies. For this reason, leaders at the summit encouraged citizens to spare no pains to exclude these bad-faith actors from public office. They cautioned the citizens of every nation not to be lulled into the illusion that democracies, even the most historically robust ones, are safe from internal sabotage. Vjosa Osmani, president of Kosovo, intently warned against appeasing authoritarians. "In the struggle between democracy and autocracy," she said, "history teaches us that appeasement of autocrats never works."

"The Way Forward," the last and longest section of the book, outlines strategies for defending democracy. Among them, Prime Minister Roosevelt Skerrit of Dominica heralded the unequivocal need for "constant effort and perpetual vigilance." Micheál Martin, prime minister of Ireland, reiterated this principle of free government, saying, "Those of us who stand firmly for democracy know that it is something that we must never take for granted. It needs constant tending and renewal. And it needs to be defended whenever and wherever it comes under pressure."

According to Ulisses Correia e Silva, prime minister of Cabo Verde, "Democracy must be protected, cared for, and enhanced with resolve and consistency."

Leaders called for untiring effort to protect democracy's sacred institutions, including election integrity, the rule of law, a free and independent media, nonviolence, equality, diversity, inclusion, economic justice, climate justice, civic virtue, and truth-seeking. Nana Akufo-Addo, president of Ghana, said democratic societies must make these commitments not for ourselves alone but "out of duty toward our children and grandchildren." Costa Rica's Carlos Alvarado Quesada quoted Mexican writer Octavio Paz, who once wrote, "A nation without free elections is a nation without a voice, without eyes, and without arms."

This summit occurred less than three months before the Russian invasion of Ukraine on February 24, 2022. President Volodymyr Zelensky of Ukraine was one of the leaders who participated in the summit. In his speech, unaware of the depth of the tragedy to come, Zelensky likewise called for global unity as democracy's best defense against authoritarian aggressions and the loss of freedoms. "We have achieved fundamental progress building our own democratic institutions and are a reliable partner for all who today are ready to come to the defense of democracy and freedom in the world," Zelensky said. "By coming together, we will make this world freer, safer, and more democratic."

How to Save Democracy, like the summit, concludes with the world leaders' call for international solidarity as the only sure way to roll back the tide of authoritarianism and advance human rights and the constitutional rule of law. "Democracy cannot be maintained nationally," said Mohamed Irfaan Ali, president of Guyana, "unless it is sustained internationally." As if speaking on behalf of an invaded country like Ukraine, Ali added, "The global chain of freedom is only as strong as its weakest link."

In the modern era, we must all—political and community leaders, heads of for-profit and nonprofit organizations, artists, writers, journalists, doctors, scientists, parents, grandparents, teachers, students, and all other citizens—embrace the democratic principles outlined at the summit and hand them down to the next generation in order for democracy to continue its march toward ever-expanding rights and freedoms for all people. As Schallenberg, former chancellor of Austria, put it, "In the end, it all boils down to one simple question: How do you want to live? As a strong believer in the democratic system, my answer is simple. I want to live in a world—I want my children and my future grandchildren to grow up in a world—where the freedom of expression, of religion or belief, the freedom of assembly, and the rights of minorities are not just noble sentiments but an everyday reality."

Words like these helped lift me out of my grief in January 2022, galvanizing me to organize and complete this book. I hope others will derive benefit from reading and sharing these inspirations on democracy, never succumbing to pessimism but instead getting involved, taking a stand, joining a group—demanding always to live in a society governed by ethical government and ethical media.

Democracy is not self-sustaining. It's the job of all of us, and our children, to carry the torch. In the words of Charles Michel, president of the European Council, at the summit, "Democracies rely on values: freedom, equality, human rights, rule of law. History has shown that these values must be nurtured, defended, fought for—with vigor and with passion every day."

I
VIRTUES OF DEMOCRACY

The Best System of Government

Democracy, as the government of the people, by the people and for the people, has been a revolution in the history of mankind.

GUY PARMELIN
Former President of Switzerland

Democracy is not negotiable. Democracy is not a commodity. It is the only system capable of ensuring in a consistent manner our individual rights and freedoms, giving each of us the possibility to live up to the best of our potential.

ALEXANDER SCHALLENBERG
Former Chancellor of Austria

It is in democracy that human beings are best fulfilled, either individually or collectively.

CARLOS VILA NOVA
President of São Tomé and Príncipe

Liberal democracies work. We know that. They work because they respect the individual. They respect each and every human being and their dignity. They respect property rights. They value enterprise. They encourage choice, and they find solutions and deliver for the common good.

SCOTT MORRISON
Prime Minister of Australia

Democracy is the most effective and sustainable route to stability, recovery, and prosperity of any country.

PHILIP J. PIERRE
Prime Minister of Saint Lucia

After the Iron Curtain came down, we were lulled into a false sense of security. We thought that with the fall of the Berlin Wall democracy would come easy and natural to every nation. We had forgotten that has never been the case. We had forgotten that liberal democracy is not the easiest answer to our current challenges. But it is the right one.

ALEXANDER DE CROO
Prime Minister of Belgium

The world's many democracies are all varied and unique. They have their own story to tell, their own imperfections to work on, and their own meaning to their people. But they also have many things in common, such as the freedom they give people to say, to do, and to choose.

URSULA VON DER LEYEN
President of the European Commission

Democracy has withstood the test of time, and, while other forms have failed, democracy stood strong. It has time and again proved its importance and impact.

MARCELO REBELO DE SOUSA
President of Portugal

In the end, it all boils down to one simple question: How do you want to live? As a strong believer in the democratic system, my answer is simple. I want to live in a world—I want my children and my future grandchildren to grow up in a world—where the freedom of expression, of religion or belief, the freedom of assembly, and the rights of minorities are not just noble sentiments but an everyday reality.

ALEXANDER SCHALLENBERG
Former Chancellor of Austria

The world deserves a much better future. It is only in democracy that we can be certain of the outcome.

STEVO PENDAROVSKI
President of North Macedonia

I remain a firm adherent of the proposition made by the great British Second World War leader, Winston Spencer Churchill, that "democracy is the worst form of government—except for all the others." We in Ghana should know because we have tried virtually all the others. . . . I am happy to state that a consensus has emerged in Ghana that the democratic form of governance is preferable—and the benefits are showing.

NANA AKUFO-ADDO
President of Ghana

Better than any other political system, [democracy] allows for the self-realization of individuals.

GUY PARMELIN
President of Switzerland

We need opportunity and prosperity, not for the few but for the many. This requires political leadership. It requires a political system with legitimate institutions and processes where people have a say. That system has a name: Democracy.

JONAS GAHR STØRE
Prime Minister of Norway

Democracy is not just an ideal: it is the best practical way of creating the atmosphere of free inquiry that allows genius to breathe.

BORIS JOHNSON
Prime Minister of the United Kingdom

It is high time to coordinate better in order to achieve stronger human rights-based systems. And democracy is the best environment for this purpose.

KLAUS IOHANNIS
President of Romania

Democracy [is] a public good because it is capable of creating conditions for the liberation of peoples from curses such as climate change, international conflict, hunger, and ignorance.

CARLOS VILA NOVA
President of São Tomé and Príncipe

What history tells us is that democracy has the infinite capacity to evolve.

JOHN BRICEÑO
Prime Minister of Belize

[Democracy] is the form of government that credibly safeguards human rights. It allows scrutiny of power, accountability and peaceful transfer of power. It creates stability, security, and economic

prosperity. And it remains the only reliable way
to facilitate social and economic equality.

MAGDALENA ANDERSSON
Prime Minister of Sweden

In an era when technological advance and therefore
economic success depends on discovery and invention,
it is no coincidence that of the ten most innovative
countries in the world, nine are liberal democracies.

BORIS JOHNSON
Prime Minister of the United Kingdom

If you want to secure our prosperity and freedoms,
there is simply no alternative to liberal democracy
and a rules-based international order.

ALEXANDER SCHALLENBERG
Former Chancellor of Austria

Democracy has become our cherished way of life, which
cannot be replaced by any other system of governance.

PHILIP J. PIERRE
Prime Minister of Saint Lucia

Core Values

We are all united by a common cause: a commitment to ensuring the freedom to openly choose our governments, to effectively address corruption, and to advance core human rights.

DAVID KABUA
President of the Marshall Islands

Democracy is participation. It's knowing how to win and how to lose within the framework governed by the rule of law.

MARIO ABDO BENÍTEZ
President of Paraguay

Our democracy is founded on the following key principles: unity, consultation, humility, and respect for the rule of law.

MOKGWEETSI E. K. MASISI
President of Botswana

Tolerance, nondiscrimination, and respect for human rights are our shared principles and values.

ULISSES CORREIA E SILVA
Prime Minister of Cabo Verde

Periodic elections, separation of powers, checks and balances, independent judiciary, and rule of law are the key features of our democracy.

SHER BAHADUR DEUBA
Prime Minister of Nepal

Democracy is a perpetual work in progress.

NIKOL PASHINYAN
Prime Minister of Armenia

As a global community for democracy, we have to stand up for the values that unite us. We have to stand for justice and the rule of law, for free speech, free assembly, a free press, freedom of religion, for all the inherent human rights of every individual.

JOSEPH R. BIDEN
President of the United States

We also know that democracy is much more than the electoral process. A solid and sound democracy implies guaranteeing democratic institutionality (the separation and independence of the powers of the state and of the branches of the state), respect for dialogue, the promotion of tolerance, freedom of expression, and political pluralism. All of these values are necessary in order to achieve peace, progress, and well-being, the pillars upon which a true democratic society is built upon.

CARLOS ALVARADO QUESADA
President of Costa Rica

We believe in a world order that favors freedom, expressed in a vibrant and pluralistic society with an open economic outlook, the rule of law and respect for territorial claims, and support for the law of the sea. We can't be casual about these important values and beliefs. They are integral to who we are as free peoples who shape our own destiny, not have them determined for us.

SCOTT MORRISON
Prime Minister of Australia

You have brought us together to discuss the only political model that permits us to defend our rights and freedoms: democracy.

EMMANUEL MACRON
President of France

Our own experience demonstrates that democratic institutions, respect for human rights, and the principle of the rule of law are the cornerstones for peace and development.

SAULI NIINISTÖ
President of Finland

The use of power must always be
tempered with wisdom.   .

LIONEL AINGIMEA
President of Nauru

Democracy—government of the people, by the
people, for the people—can at times be fragile. But
it also is inherently resilient. It is capable of self-
correction, and it is capable of self-improvement.

JOSEPH R. BIDEN
President of the United States

Democracy is a work in progress, requiring
constant effort and perpetual vigilance.

ROOSEVELT SKERRIT
Prime Minister of Dominica

The government of Guyana is fully committed
to strengthening the foundations and pillars
of democracy to ensure that, at all times in the
future, the will of the electorate is upheld in

free, fair, and transparent elections, and that the
independence of the judiciary is maintained.

MOHAMED IRFAAN ALI
President of Guyana

Our commitment to democracy is pursued
with inclusion and scrutiny of civil society and
nongovernmental organizations as well as a free
press. . . . Like any other system of government,
however, democracy's true test lies in its ability
to effectively address the needs of the people. . . .
Democratic countries must therefore continually
improve citizens' security; increase access to
education, health and economic opportunities;
reduce inequality; protect human and environmental
rights and diversity; improve anti-corruption
frameworks; and maintain the rule of law.

ANDREW HOLNESS
Prime Minister of Jamaica

It is our duty to step up and highlight the values
which have allowed our societies to emerge and

prosper—and renew our commitment to them,
all while protecting the most vulnerable.

XAVIER BETTEL
President of Luxembourg

Strengthening democracy, even under adverse
conditions, is about three things. First, having strong
governance institutions carrying out their constitutional
mandate when the situation demands it. Second, having
political leaders use their platforms to engage citizens
in actively holding those institutions accountable. And
third, protecting the rights of citizens and enforcing
consequences legally on those who violate them.

LAZARUS MCCARTHY CHAKWERA
President of Malawi

A healthy democracy needs to have the necessary
checks and balances that promote accountability and
transparency, including an independent judiciary,
freedom of expression, and well-functioning
institutions that make our democracy work.

JACINDA ARDERN
Prime Minister of New Zealand

Without a vibrant civil society democracy dies.
Democratic participation must be inclusive, safe, and
nondiscriminating. Freedoms of expression, association,
and assembly are cornerstones in democracy.

JONAS GAHR STØRE
Prime Minister of Norway

The challenges of democracy also demand
guaranteeing the rule of law, the balance of powers,
the independence of justice administration
systems, and freedom of press and speech.

PEDRO CASTILLO
President of Peru

For us, the building of a good society, responsive
to the needs of all of our people, especially
the most vulnerable, has always been at the
foundation of our understanding as to what
constitutes a successful democracy.

MIA AMOR MOTTLEY
Prime Minister of Barbados

The strengthening of democracy, defending against authoritarianism, and fighting corruption is a trilogy of ideals hinged on the respect for human rights and the dignity of human life. All three are grounded in an imperative that respects and recognizes that every life is imbued with intrinsic value. All who govern must ensure that the governed are empowered with every opportunity to maximize this intrinsic value and achieve self-actualization, the promise of a true participatory democracy.

TIMOTHY HARRIS
Prime Minister of Saint Kitts and Nevis

Democracy is never achieved. It is a work in constant progress.

GUY PARMELIN
President of Switzerland

Lately we are facing crises of trust in democratic institutions. What is equally troubling is low levels of political and legal culture. So our effort for democracy starts with dialogue and mutual respect, without exclusion and hate speech.

BORUT PAHOR
President of Slovenia

While democracy is not perfect, it is perfectible. And that is the difference between democracy and autocracy. In democracies, you can criticize. You can protest. And you can freely discuss opposing ideas. That's freedom. So let's stand up for it. Let's take up the challenge together.

URSULA VON DER LEYEN
President of the European Commission

The Will of the People

Ultimately, the strength and legitimacy
of democracy comes from the people.
Ultimate power resides in the people.

JOHN BRICEÑO
Prime Minister of Belize

It is democracy which vests the supreme authority
to the people to directly or indirectly, through
free and fair elections, elect our leaders.

LIONEL AINGIMEA
President of Nauru

No two democracies are the same. No matter where democracy has taken root on this planet, it's unique in its own way. But every democracy has many things in common. I would argue that they have the most important thing in common: they give power to the people.

CHARLES MICHEL
President of the European Council

Jamaica is proud of our seventy-six years of universal adult suffrage and uninterrupted democratic election of governments. Democracy, however, is more than the mechanics of free elections. It is a commitment by the state to respect the will of the people—every day.

ANDREW HOLNESS
Prime Minister of Jamaica

President Abraham Lincoln put it aptly: Democracy is government of the people, by the people, for the people.

PHILIP J. PIERRE
Prime Minister of Saint Lucia

Hearing and respecting the voice and place of all the peoples of the world is central to modern democracy.

ROOSEVELT SKERRIT
Prime Minister of Dominica

Democracy in Taiwan isn't just *for* the people but *with* the people.

AUDREY TANG
Digital Minister of Taiwan

The electoral framework should truly reflect the will of the people.

PHILIP J. PIERRE
Prime Minister of Saint Lucia

In our country, Zambia, earlier this year, we saw a democratic revival. The leading actors were the people of Zambia. Young and old, male and female, rich and poor, from all creeds, races and tribes, they are the heroes of this story.

HAKAINDE HICHILEMA
President of Zambia

Out of Athens more than twenty-five hundred years ago, there came a simple and beautiful idea: that people are neither passive nor powerless but free citizens with a right to participate in the governance of their country.

BORIS JOHNSON
Prime Minister of the United Kingdom

Democracy is as much a psychological process as it is an economic or judicial process. People need to have choices, and they must be free to make their own decisions.

PHILIP J. PIERRE
Prime Minister of Saint Lucia

Our communal culture ingrained in our people the notion . . . that the pathway to leadership is through service. I believe this is the same concept of democracy promoted in the values embodied in the Universal Declaration of Human Rights, which states, "The will of the people shall be the basis of the authority of government."

FIAMĒ NAOMI MATA'AFA
Prime Minister of Samoa

Our governance mantra, "Putting people first,"
is a pledge to the people of Saint Lucia.

PHILIP J. PIERRE
Prime Minister of Saint Lucia

The dynamism and vitality of a democracy
. . . takes root in society and in the passion
of a people who believe in their values.

CARLOS VILA NOVA
President of São Tomé and Príncipe

Freedom and Rights

Democracy is in the fabric of our society; it is deeply entrenched in our historic struggle for freedom and human rights.

VJOSA OSMANI
President of Kosovo

The need for nations to intensify efforts in making human rights a reality for all peoples across the world, without discrimination, particularly in the context of the COVID-19 pandemic, cannot be overemphasized.

MOKGWEETSI E. K. MASISI
President of Botswana

We must, as servants of our countries, envisage how to promote respect for human rights by succeeding in the quest to regulate, civilize, and create mechanisms for order around us which protects harmony, guarantees safe possession, and allows society to develop.

LIONEL AINGIMEA
President of Nauru

In an age of new and emerging technology, it is also vital that we work together and that we put human rights at the center of our approach. That means that governments must work alongside civil society and the private sector in more open formats, finding durable, collaborative global solutions.

JACINDA ARDERN
Prime Minister of New Zealand

Ireland's commitment to supporting democracy and human rights at home and internationally—and to combat authoritarianism and global corruption—is unwavering.

MICHEÁL MARTIN
Prime Minister of Ireland

Peace, Cooperation, and Dignity

Democracy is the greatest guarantor of peace.

ALBERTO FERNÁNDEZ
President of Argentina

We must never forget that democracy is not simply a monolithic institutional construct. It is about people. And this is why we must commit always to seeing each other, to hearing each other, and to caring for each other. If we can do this, then we can give breath to democracy each and every day.

MIA AMOR MOTTLEY
Prime Minister of Barbados

Democracy is hard. We all know that. It works best with consensus and cooperation.

JOSEPH R. BIDEN
President of the United States

Our culture and traditions mean we take collective responsibility for each other. Our core values of respect, dignity, love, protection, and service guide social interaction.

FIAMĒ NAOMI MATA'AFA
Prime Minister of Samoa

Solidarity and cooperation are needed to launch effective and efficient responses to the threats against the democratic system.

IVÁN DUQUE
President of Colombia

If we do not engage in respectful dialogue, we only deepen riffs and polarization in and between our societies. A meaningful dialogue is a precondition for constructive cooperation, and cooperation is the only way of reaching peaceful solutions to all problems.

BORUT PAHOR
President of Slovenia

If we are to embrace the path of peace, progress, and prosperity, we must be alive to the risks of complacency, and continue to listen carefully to the voice of the people. After all, the word itself, *democracy*, from the Greek *demos* and *kratos*, means the people's strength or power. We forget that at our peril.

KYRIAKOS MITSOTAKIS
Prime Minister of Greece

Let's build democracy through respectful dialogue and constructive cooperation.

BORUT PAHOR
President of Slovenia

Swiss foreign policy has a constitutional mandate to promote democracy. Our approach is a principled one, not against someone, but for democracy not only because we are convince that democracy can bring justice and freedom at the individual level but also peace, stability, and prosperity among nations.

GUY PARMELIN
President of Switzerland

My administration understands the natural inclination of people, irrespective of race, class, creed, or religion, to be free to live in peace, love, and dignity.

PHILIP J. PIERRE
Prime Minister of Saint Lucia

Some in the past have argued that [democracy] is impractical or even dangerous. But history has shown that democracy can bring justice, social stability, peace, freedom, and economic prosperity. Better than any other political system, it allows for the self-realization of individuals.

GUY PARMELIN
President of Switzerland

A democracy needs peace to survive.

RODRIGO DUTERTE
President of the Philippines

[Democracy] is a system based on seeking compromise and consensus, a system that gives nuanced answers to complex issues. Democracy's biggest enemies are simplicity and black-and-white thinking. That is why, in Belgium, we are standing up for this complex, nuanced democratic model.

ALEXANDER DE CROO
Prime Minister of Belgium

Democracy is not a stable condition. It is a coming together of antagonistic social forces and individuals willing to compromise for the greater good.

GUY PARMELIN
President of Switzerland

While each one of our countries faces real challenges, we also know that democracy remains the most effective way to tackle those challenges and to advance human dignity.

ANTONY BLINKEN
US Secretary of State

[Democracy is] the best way to unleash human potential and defend human dignity and solve big problems.

JOSEPH R. BIDEN
President of the United States

This is the time to renew our faith in the values and principles that uplifted free peoples everywhere, in the equality of all people, in human dignity expressed through freedom of speech, freedom of religion, and freedom of association—in the rule of law and the ballot box and a free press.

SCOTT MORRISON
Prime Minister of Australia

Let us work continuously to deliver on the rich promise of democracy—that all citizens can live in peace with dignity and are afforded equal opportunities to fulfill their destiny.

JOHN BRICEÑO
Prime Minister of Belize

At the core, all of our democratic institutions are legitimate dispute-settlement mechanisms.

SEBASTIÁN PIÑERA
President of Chile

Above all, democracy is dialogue, and dialogue must take place in a harmonious environment.

ALBERTO FERNÁNDEZ
President of Argentina

We in Caricom affirm the enduring values of dialogue, diplomacy, and the peaceful resolution of differences in helping to chart the way forward in our dynamic modern times.

KEITH ROWLEY
Prime Minister of Trinidad and Tobago

Disagreements are welcome in a democratic society. But they must be resolved peacefully and within the rule of law.

SEBASTIÁN PIÑERA
President of Chile

Sustainable peace needs strong democracies.

EDI RAMA
Prime Minister of Albania

Engine of Progress

We also know from the evidence of human history
that democracies are the engine room of change,
be it social, economic or political. Democracies are
where innovation and enterprise flourish freely.

SCOTT MORRISON
Prime Minister of Australia

We have seen the power democracy has to create
momentum and a belief that positive change is possible.

URSULA VON DER LEYEN
President of the European Commission

We have seen how democracy can be unwieldy, as we
all know it can be. But we have also seen how it can be a

powerful means to translate the people's priorities into policy and create a solid foundation for national unity.

AIYAZ SAYED-KHAIYUM
Acting Prime Minister of Fiji

Ultimately, democracy is best placed to deliver the most equitable outcomes for social issues, large and small.

MARK RUTTE
Prime Minister of the Netherlands

The India story has one clear message to the world. That democracy can deliver, that democracy has delivered, and that democracy will continue to deliver.

NARENDRA MODI
Prime Minister of India

Democracies can be loud, but the engine of change is always loud.

SCOTT MORRISON
Prime Minister of Australia

II

CHALLENGES
AND THREATS

Complacency

We must not take democracy for granted,
and we must relentlessly protect it.

VJOSA OSMANI
President of Kosovo

We can't be complacent about our democracies
and the values that sustain them.

SCOTT MORRISON
Prime Minister of Australia

We need to remember the value of what
we often take for granted: human rights
and freedoms, peace and security.

MAIA SANDU
President of Moldova

Democracy and freedom can be like the air. When you have it, you take it for granted. But when you don't have it, you miss it, and you realize how important it is and how hard it can be to regain it.

SEBASTIÁN PIÑERA
President of Chile

We cannot take our freedoms for granted. Aware that people yearn for freedom and empowerment, some autocracies are relentless in their efforts to undermine democratic systems.

EGILS LEVITS
President of Latvia

We want to renew the commitment to a responsible, democratic and safe tech development, because we can never take democracy for granted.

METTE FREDERIKSEN
Prime Minister of Denmark

We should not take for granted something that needs
to be built together—again and again, every day.

MARCELO REBELO DE SOUSA
President of Portugal

We cannot take democracy for granted, but nor
should we waver in our faith that trusting the people
is the surest route to national unity and success.

BORIS JOHNSON
Prime Minister of the United Kingdom

Thank you again, President Biden, for providing
us this opportunity to reflect on the importance
of democracy. We must never take it for granted.
And thank you for giving us this platform from
which to renew our strong commitments to
build better and more democratic societies.

SEBASTIÁN PIÑERA
President of Chile

Technology and the Digital Revolution

The democratic conversation is changing. New technologies and large tech companies are increasingly setting the stage for the democratic dialogue.

METTE FREDERIKSEN
Prime Minister of Denmark

Citizens come together online, speaking with one voice. This is no ordinary power. It is a special and unprecedented power. But like all new and powerful tools, our digital transformation also brings challenges to our democracies.

CHARLES MICHEL
President of the European Council

Strengthening of contacts and better infrastructural connectivity are the starting point for a higher quality of life for citizens, which facilitates dialogue on respect for democratic values.

ALEKSANDAR VUČIĆ
President of Serbia

Big Tech has amassed enormous power. But not all have shown the willingness to accept the matching responsibility. Their market dominance and data control give them enormous influence over our democratic process.

CHARLES MICHEL
President of the European Council

The growing complexity of issues we are confronted with sometimes seems to favor technocratic solutions lacking democratic foundations.

GUY PARMELIN
President of Switzerland

Governments must reclaim the steering wheel of digital development. We need to make technology work for us. For our democracy, not the opposite.

METTE FREDERIKSEN
Prime Minister of Denmark

Today more than ever, our democracies and the lives of our citizens are defined by the digital transformation. This transformation presents both huge opportunities but also risks for our democracies. We, in Europe, strive to place democratic values at the heart of our digital transformation, a transformation focused on people and their well-being. We believe that this approach can be a global model for a free, secure, values-based internet.

CHARLES MICHEL
President of the European Council

Along with important opportunities, digitalization of our world poses an additional challenge to democracy. My claim is that there is reason for optimism. Democracies are resilient.

GUY PARMELIN
President of Switzerland

During the pandemic, we have witnessed the tremendous power of the internet to bring people together. . . . Crucially, the internet also has the power to hold politicians and public institutions accountable.

CHARLES MICHEL
President of the European Council

Our societies are also going through a continuous digital transformation, a process that we must ensure leads to more equal societies.

KATRÍN JAKOBSDÓTTIR
Prime Minister of Iceland

We have a clear vision for a digitally transformed Europe by 2030. A transformation that puts people, and our planet, at the heart of our digital future. We want to be a global leader in promoting an open, interoperable, reliable and secure internet.

CHARLES MICHEL
President of the European Council

We need democracies to set the rules of the game and work for safe and accessible global digital infrastructure.

KAJA KALLAS
Prime Minister of Estonia

New technologies will revolutionize our way of life and transform societies. By working together, we can provide innovative leadership. We can make sure new technologies support democratization and human rights.

MARK RUTTE
Prime Minister of the Netherlands

We want an internet underpinned by rules that protect our citizens. And we want to help our partners become freer and more democratic, because democracy and openness place the greatest freedom in the hands of people.

CHARLES MICHEL
President of the European Council

Democracy should be reinforced—not undermined— in the digital domain. Through the Digital Public Goods Alliance, we will contribute to inclusion by investing in good digital public infrastructure.

JONAS GAHR STØRE
Prime Minister of Norway

Besides building dedicated centers to deal with
hybrid threats at home, we need to come up with
a democratic global framework to enforce social
media platforms' responsibility and accountability.

ZUZANA ČAPUTOVÁ
President of Slovakia

Our digital future is bursting with possibilities beyond
our imaginations. Global data is today's equivalent of
yesterday's carbon. And it's why today we must not
repeat the mistakes of the past. We must choose this
powerful new resource wisely and sustainably. We must
ensure this vast potential [of digital transformation] is
harnessed for the good—good for our citizens, good
for our societies, and good for our democracies.

CHARLES MICHEL
President of the European Council

Individuals around the world now have the possibility
to exercise their rights to freedom of opinion and
expression online—and have access to information
from different sources in an unprecedented way.
The international community must work together
to ensure that these new technologies can serve

as tools to protect and promote human rights, fundamental freedoms, and democratic values.

ESTEBAN MOCTEZUMA
Ambassador of Mexico

We are equally working to strengthen people's digital literacy. Their democratic rights must be guaranteed online in the same way as they are offline.

CHARLES MICHEL
President of the European Council

Democratic Recession

The Summit for Democracy comes at a critical
time in which our model of democracy,
underpinned by human rights and the rule of
law, is being challenged across the globe.

JACINDA ARDERN
Prime Minister of New Zealand

We have seen a democratic recession in recent years.

ANTONY BLINKEN
US Secretary of State

In recent years, we have sadly witnessed some
serious backlash in democracy, human rights,
and gender equality around the world. This trend

must be reversed, inter alia, with the help of independent media and strong civil society.

KATRÍN JAKOBSDÓTTIR
Prime Minister of Iceland

We stand at an inflection point in our history . . . the choices we make, in my view, in this moment, are going to fundamentally determine the direction our world is going to take in the coming decades. Will we allow the backward slide of rights and democracy to continue unchecked? Or will we together, together, have a vision and the vision—not just a vision, *the* vision—and courage to once more lead the march of human progress and human freedom forward? I believe we can do that and we will—if we have faith in ourselves and in our democracies and then each other.

JOSEPH R. BIDEN
President of the United States

We all are witnessing the weakening of the "immune system" of democracies worldwide.

STEVO PENDAROVSKI
President of North Macedonia

This is a unique time for democracy. Marked by extremes and extremist positions, democratic institutions have become weakened . . . this is something we must examine and address with all due seriousness.

ALBERTO FERNÁNDEZ
President of Argentina

The long democratic recession is deepening. The imminent risks are clear, particularly for those who have fought for democracy to be consolidated and cherished during the twentieth century.

MAIA SANDU
President of Moldova

Nowadays democracy is not a given any more. Neither as a system nor as a goal.

ALEXANDER SCHALLENBERG
Former Chancellor of Austria

We see new geopolitical, technological, and economic conditions threatening democratic institutions globally.

GITANAS NAUSĖDA
President of Lithuania

We are at yet another crossroads in history where democracy is challenged more than ever by concurrent crisis, lack of trust in the capacity of the state to address people's needs, and poor vision on behalf of political leaders for how to protect democracy.

MAIA SANDU

President of Moldova

Many democracies are now facing profound challenges. Some previously democratic countries seem to be succumbing to authoritarian ideas. Others are struggling to preserve the independence of the judiciary.

MARK RUTTE

Prime Minister of the Netherlands

Corruption

A society free from corruption is a
fundamental human right.

KEITH ROWLEY
*Prime Minister of Trinidad
and Tobago*

There is no bigger enemy to democracy than corruption.

MOON JAE-IN
President of the Republic of Korea

Corruption is a main cause of inequality,
poverty, frustration, violence, migration, and
serious social conflicts around the world.

ESTEBAN MOCTEZUMA
Ambassador of Mexico

We know corruption corrodes democratic
institutions and helps hostile autocratic
regimes to gain illicit influence.

GITANAS NAUSĖDA
President of Lithuania

Corruption destroys democracy and the rule of law
because it hinders accountability and transparency.

CHANDRIKAPERSAD SANTOKHI
President of Suriname

We need to also reflect why there's so much citizen
mistrust toward democracy. Some of the errors that
have been made, including impunity which reflects
a weak judiciary and corruption that seeps into
all branches of government, is just a subset of the
problems that affect the Latin American continent.

MARIO ABDO BENÍTEZ
President of Paraguay

The mark of our success in the war against corruption
is to continue developing accountable institutions and

to grow local, organic solutions demanding exercise of integrity by the current and also future generations.

UHURU KENYATTA
President of Kenya

Corruption erodes democratic institutions and undermines public trust and confidence.

JOHN BRICEŇO
Prime Minister of Belize

Transnational crime, corruption, violence, and drug trafficking are some of the current threats to democracy.

IVÁN DUQUE
President of Colombia

Autocratic regimes tend to store their stolen assets in Western banks and properties, thereby facilitating corruption in our democracies. This chain must be broken.

EGILS LEVITS
President of Latvia

To ensure that we deliver strong, stable, and mature democracies for our future generations, it is imperative to build a strong foundation for good institutions today. This is why one of the prime commitments of my government is to fight corruption and increase accountability.

IBRAHIM MOHAMED SOLI
President of Maldives

Demagogues and Authoritarians

Today democracy is being threatened from within.
Some say that democracy is in crisis. . . . Fake
news, traveling fast through new forms of digital
media and social networking services, is spreading
hatred, populism, and extremism and even inciting
people to refuse to be vaccinated. Nevertheless,
we still have not found appropriate measures to
deter these acts because they might collide with
a democratic value—freedom of expression.

MOON JAE-IN
President of the Republic of Korea

During the last centuries, strengthening and protecting
our democracies meant shielding them mostly from

foreign threats or violent military coups. The last
decades, however, have shown us that today the most
recurrent threats to democracy come from within.

SEBASTIÁN PIÑERA
President of Chile

We must remain vigilant of those who have more love
for power than for democracy, for they will not hesitate
to employ or justify violence if it serves their goals.

SEBASTIÁN PIÑERA
President of Chile

In the last decade, on all continents, even in
established democracies, we have witnessed a
rise of populism and authoritarian tendencies
challenging and making democracy vulnerable.
. . . Revitalizing democracy is essential to handle
this unprecedented challenge of our lifetime.

STEVO PENDAROVSKI
President of North Macedonia

Democracy has all the credentials to prevail
over authoritarianism, and the community

of democratic nations is obliged to promote
and protect it. The alternative is going back
in history marked by destruction and the
immense suffering of millions of people.

STEVO PENDAROVSKI
President of North Macedonia

In the struggle between democracy and autocracy,
history teaches us that appeasement of autocrats
never works. Today is more than a summit; it is our
collective voice rejecting autocratic tendencies, and it
is our collective voice standing up for democracy.

VJOSA OSMANI
President of Kosovo

Let us use this wonderful opportunity to
grow in our understanding of how democracy
works and how tyranny happens.

GITANAS NAUSĖDA
President of Lithuania

This is also a time of resolve because we are living
in a time of great uncertainty. The rules-based

order that has served us so well for so long, based
on those important liberal democratic principles
that have underpinned our stability and our
prosperity, is under threat from growing autocracy
in so many countries around the world, from
rapid military modernization, the undermining
of international law, from this disinformation,
foreign interference, and malicious cyber threats.

SCOTT MORRISON
Prime Minister of Australia

When politicians place themselves above the
law, confidence in democracy erodes.

JONAS GAHR STØRE
Prime Minister of Norway

Many of our societies appear less protective today
of their pluralism and more accepting of populism.
My experience has been that populism thrives
most easily where people have lost trust in their
governments, parliaments, and courts, where are large
numbers of citizens feel deprived of opportunities,
[and] minorities have not been integrated into wider
society. . . . The same thing befalls democracy as it

does security, freedom, health, and everything that, having been conquered, we now take for granted.

MARCELO REBELO DE SOUSA
President of Portugal

The absence of democracy in the Pacific—and in the rest of the world—will result in instability and chaos. Left unchecked, authoritarian powers pose a very real threat to the world.

SURANGEL S. WHIPPS JR.
President of Palau

Poland is aware of the fact that supporting democracy has its price attached. It is paying this price today with our border guards, police and army guarding the eastern border of the European Union against a dictator's revenge, against tyranny and contempt for humanity.

ANDRZEJ DUDA
President of Poland

In our bid to consolidate our democracy, we are facing multiple challenges. The biggest challenge for us comes in the form of military threats to our security. Fighting for democracy at home is yet another challenge. That challenge is compounded when threats arise from beyond our borders.

NIKOL PASHINYAN
Prime Minister of Armenia

Power is not to be abused to the extent where the majority use it for authoritarian purposes. Powers given to the leaders are to be appropriately utilized. Otherwise, as Lord Acton said, "Power tends to corrupt, and absolute power corrupts absolutely."

LIONEL AINGIMEA
President of Nauru

We have also learned that the erosion of democracy and the silent rise of autocracy can spread just as fast.

URSULA VON DER LEYEN
President of the European Commission

We live in a time of increasing instability, with growing authoritarianism and too many losing confidence in our democratic institutions.

JUSTIN TRUDEAU
Prime Minister of Canada

We, the countries of the democratic world, are all
under the same threat from those who see democracy
as an obstacle toward their unscrupulous goals.

ANDREJ PLENKOVIĆ
Prime Minister of Croatia

We know how painful it is when a small
group takes unlimited power and imposes
a single vision on all of society.

URSULA VON DER LEYEN
President of the European Commission

Despite the progress we have made, democratic
institutions in Africa are facing growing threats
characterized by military coups and manipulated
constitutional amendments to elongate tenures.

MUHAMMADU BUHARI
President of Nigeria

The threats against our democracies are increasing,
and authoritarianism and corruption are on the rise.

NAFTALI BENNETT
Prime Minister of Israel

We all know tyrants hate free speech and try to destroy it whenever they get the chance.

GITANAS NAUSĖDA
President of Lithuania

In recent years, Greece, the birthplace of democracy, has experienced firsthand the divisive politics, failed promises, and empty rhetoric of both Far Left and Far Right populism—and has rejected both. ... Our success has been in our ability to listen— listen to legitimate grievances and concerns that fed the well of anger—and then act upon those concerns. As such, we were and remain determined to focus on the issues that really matter to people.

KYRIAKOS MITSOTAKIS
Prime Minister of Greece

Developed democracies must avoid being breeding grounds for anti-government movements that threaten our nascent democracies.

MUHAMMADU BUHARI
President of Nigeria

The strengthening of democracy is part of
the bulwark against authoritarian rule.

TIMOTHY HARRIS
Prime Minister of Saint Kitts and Nevis

If we are to strengthen democracy, then we must
also face down the continued threat posed not
just by authoritarianism but by populism too.

KYRIAKOS MITSOTAKIS
Prime Minister of Greece

We must strengthen our democracy and
defend it against authoritarianism.

GEORGE WEAH
President of Liberia

Disinformation

The historic roots of attack on democracy have been superseded. Tyranny can creep in not just via the bullet but via misinformation, via false advertising, the fake profile or vote— all of it fractures trust within our societies.

PHILIP DAVIS
Prime Minister of the Bahamas

Democracy and the rules-based international order can, however, be challenged by new threats. One of these challenges is the evolving rule of digital media. . . . These issues include the spread of disinformation, or misinformation, online. . . . If they are not addressed, these challenges will contribute to a gradual erosion of democratic spaces.

PRAVIND KUMAR JUGNAUTH
Prime Minister of Mauritius

Technology holds great potential to make democracy stronger. Technology connects us and enables people to engage in society. And with digital solutions we are able to do things smarter, faster and better. Yet at the same time, the digital age is also a challenge to democracy. When a small number of companies have the power to influence our democratic conversation, when facts are being put into question, and fake news spreads, when disinformation campaigns are used to attack democratic institutions and elections, we need a joint political answer.

METTE FREDERIKSEN
Prime Minister of Denmark

Misinformation is not random. It is designed and coordinated with a very clear-cut intent, which is to destabilize and sow despair and disappointment.

MARIO ABDO BENÍTEZ
President of Paraguay

One could not have thought a more appropriate moment to launch this initiative, for democracy is today confronted by serious challenges and new threats to the point that we could say that there is a war declared against democracy. . . . New and nontraditional threats have emerged, primarily targeting democratic institutions. . . . Democracies across the globe are now faced with hybrid warfare methods that include cyberattacks, disinformation, and targeted economic pressures and coercions. . . . Democracies are also attacked from within. Polarization, fake news, and hate speech not only fuel internal divisions but also undermine public institutions and democratic processes, including trust in elections or in the media, two of the pillars of democracy.

SALOME ZOURABICHVILI
President of Georgia

It is vitally important to build resilience against disinformation. Social networks have become the main source of disinformation and fake news, which facilitates populism.

EGILS LEVITS
President of Latvia

Corruption, or disinformation campaigns, are subversive to the smooth function of democratic institutions. In addition, even more dangerously, they erode citizens' trust in the democratic system and international law, as such.

ANDREJ BABIŠ
Prime Minister of the Czech Republic

Disinformation skews the way we see democracy and perceive the world.

URSULA VON DER LEYEN
President of the European Commission

We will do our best to protect human rights, to promote media freedom, and fight disinformation— and to make technology inclusive.

SAULI NIINISTÖ
President of Finland

Today most threats against democracy come from within—from elected leaders who act in breach of democratic principles, embrace corruption, and disregard human rights. The threat is often amplified by disinformation.

JONAS GAHR STØRE
Prime Minister of Norway

Of no lesser importance is the need to analyze in a more rigorous way the issue of disinformation as a tool to destabilize democracy. Fake news can be taken for the truth in just a matter of minutes.

MARIO ABDO BENÍTEZ
President of Paraguay

I urge our friends in the host democracies of these technology giants to take appropriate steps to rein in these insidious threats which do so much to poison the discourse of all of our countries.

PHILIP DAVIS
Prime Minister of the Bahamas

III

THE WAY FORWARD

Constant Effort

Democracies rely on values: freedom, equality, human rights, rule of law. History has shown that these values must be nurtured, defended, fought for—with vigor and with passion every day.

CHARLES MICHEL
President of the European Council

Democracy is the result of women and men demanding fair and equitable sharing of power. It is something that we must continue to work for—each and every day.

MAGDALENA ANDERSSON
Prime Minister of Sweden

Democracy is much more than a government.
It is a way of living in freedom, in a state of law
where we all fit in. It is a universal value system
which requires our effort and exemplary character
to successfully combat those who oppose it.

PEDRO SÁNCHEZ
President of Spain

Democracy needs champions.

JOSEPH R. BIDEN
President of the United States

Democracy requires constant vigilance in maintaining
and strengthening its institutions and principles.

ANDREW HOLNESS
Prime Minister of Jamaica

We all must play our part in the untiring effort to protect
the integrity of our democratic systems for the future.

MICHEÁL MARTIN
Prime Minister of Ireland

American democracy is an ongoing struggle to live up to our highest ideals and to heal our divisions and recommit ourselves to the founding idea of our nation as captured in our Declaration of Independence.

JOSEPH R. BIDEN
President of the United States

An engaged society is the most reliable barrier against the erosion of our freedoms.

SURANGEL S. WHIPPS JR.
President of Palau

We need to champion democracy. Let's not forget that democracy is always a work in progress. We need to cherish and defend it. We need to reform it for the future generations.

MARCELO REBELO DE SOUSA
President of Portugal

We acknowledge that there is no perfect democracy. Thus, it is always in human civilization a work in progress.

RALPH GONSALVES
Prime Minister of Saint Vincent and the Grenadines

Democracy doesn't happen by accident. We have to renew it with each generation.

JOSEPH R. BIDEN
President of the United States

We are aware, however, that no democracy is perfect. We are part of a globalized world which influences us. That is why democracy must be protected, cared for, and enhanced with resolve and consistency.

ULISSES CORREIA E SILVA
Prime Minister of Cabo Verde

Only strong political will makes meaningful change happen.

GITANAS NAUSĖDA
President of Lithuania

Through hard work, we have been able to steer free from authoritarianism and implement strong measures to consolidate our democratic gains.

IBRAHIM MOHAMED SOLI
President of Maldives

Those of us who stand firmly for democracy know that it is something that we must never take for granted. It needs constant tending and renewal. And it needs to be defended whenever and wherever it comes under pressure.

MICHEÁL MARTIN
Prime Minister of Ireland

The institutions of a participatory democracy are not self-sustaining, and consequently they must be buttressed by the deliberate positioning of institutional safeguards.

TIMOTHY HARRIS
Prime Minister of Saint Kitts and Nevis

Renewing our democracy and strengthening our democratic institutions requires constant effort.

JOSEPH R. BIDEN
President of the United States

We have to work hard and ensure that democracy delivers.

JOKO WIDODO
President of Indonesia

Democracy must be promoted wherever it is gaining a foothold. Democracy must be defended wherever it is under threat.

SAULI NIINISTÖ
President of Finland

Democracy is not something we can take for granted. It requires constant renewal in order to face the challenges of our time. For each of us, that work starts at home.

JUSTIN TRUDEAU
Prime Minister of Canada

To quote former US President John F. Kennedy,
"Democracy is never a final achievement.
It is a call to an untiring effort."

MICHEÁL MARTIN
Prime Minister of Ireland

Citizen participation is essential as
a pillar of our democracy.

LAURENTINO CORTIZO COHEN
President of Panama

Democracy requires constant renewal and
protection as well as engagement at the
domestic and the international level.

ROOSEVELT SKERRIT
Prime Minister of Dominica

We are in a constant and consistent process of reform
and will continue implementing the necessary changes
to defend democracy both locally and internationally.

ROBERT ABELA
Prime Minister of Malta

The path to stable democracy is never smooth in any country. Development of democracy is never straightforward.

KISHIDA FUMIO
Prime Minister of Japan

Not only do we need to build on our democratic traditions but we must be constantly vigilant to avoid erosion of the progress made thus far.

PHILIP J. PIERRE
Prime Minister of Saint Lucia

Democracy is not a byword for harmony. Its institutions can be strained by tensions and competing interests.

MARK RUTTE
Prime Minister of the Netherlands

Slovakia has had its democratic hesitations. Painful as they may be, they taught us that for democracy to survive it must be a constant process of self-improvement. Let's strive for this together.

ZUZANA ČAPUTOVÁ
President of Slovakia

There is much we can learn from each other. We all need to constantly improve our democratic practices and systems. And we all need to continuously enhance inclusion, transparency, human dignity, responsive grievance redressal, and decentralization of power.

NARENDRA MODI
Prime Minister of India

Youth activists, community leaders, and journalists play an integral role in the protection and promotion of human rights, democracies, and the rule of law.

XAVIER BETTEL
President of Luxembourg

Freedom from Prejudice, Discrimination, and Violence

No country can boast of being a democracy unless its institutions, policies, legal systems, and practices stamp out racial prejudice and institutionalized racism.

ROOSEVELT SKERRIT
Prime Minister of Dominica

In the area of human rights advancement, an essential component is to ensure the safety and security of communities, individuals, and institutions against anti-Semitism, xenophobia, radicalization, and hate speech.

KLAUS IOHANNIS
President of Romania

Rather than erect glass ceilings, a genuine democracy must empower marginalized groups, like women, to take part.

AIYAZ SAYED-KHAIYUM
Acting Prime Minister of Fiji

I am proud to share that we are in the process of appointing a national coordinator of policies combating racism, anti-Semitism, and hatred of LGBTIA+ people. This position is part of our national approach to the prevention of discrimination and to promote the respect of diversity, two fundamental notions if we want our societies to be peaceful [and] inclusive.

XAVIER BETTEL
President of Luxembourg

As Isaac Asimov once wrote: "Violence is the last refuge of the incompetent." And democracy has no room for such incompetence.

SEBASTIÁN PIÑERA
President of Chile

The contemporary challenges to democracy
in the Caribbean include poverty and material
privation, the threats of recolonization and
hegemonic domination, the misuse and abuse of
global information technologies, the weaknesses
of certain critical democratic institutions of
governance, the corrosive dangers of corruption,
the rise of transnational and internal criminality,
including violence against women, and, in several
countries in our hemisphere and elsewhere, the
challenge of ethnic or racial discrimination.

RALPH GONSALVES
*Prime Minister of Saint Vincent
and the Grenadines*

Adherence to democracy and the rule of law must be
aligned with economic and social progress in conditions
of nondiscrimination, equity, and equal opportunities.

MOHAMED IRFAAN ALI
President of Guyana

Today it is more important than ever not only that
we abstain from justifying political violence but
also that we at our national levels, but also at the
international one, stand ready and willing to denounce

and condemn those who excuse or use violence as a means to impose their idea over the rest of society.

SEBASTIÁN PIÑERA
President of Chile

We declare zero tolerance to gender based violence, sexual abuse, exploitation of children and teenagers.

ULISSES CORREIA E SILVA
Prime Minister of Cabo Verde

Diversity, Inclusion, and Equality

Liberal democracy is as much about
protecting minorities, protecting diversity,
as it is about the power of the majority.

ALEXANDER DE CROO
Prime Minister of Belgium

Our commitment to enriching democracy is
anchored in socially inclusive national strategies,
reflecting the will of the people—their consent and
participation—while focusing on long-term goals.

MOKGWEETSI E. K. MASISI
President of Botswana

Liberal democracy is not about having "a strong leader." It is about strong leadership. It is my deep conviction that strong leadership is based on diversity and on inclusion.

ALEXANDER DE CROO
Prime Minister of Belgium

Our guiding principle is that no one should be left aside in the exercise of fundamental rights and freedoms.

ALEKSANDAR VUČIĆ
President of Serbia

We consider a free, open, and inclusive economy to be the right approach to democratic governance.

PRAVIND KUMAR JUGNAUTH
Prime Minister of Mauritius

In our contract with the people, we pledge to govern our country by the principles of inclusiveness [and] equity, strictly underpinned by the principles of good government.

PHILIP J. PIERRE
Prime Minister of Saint Lucia

Serbia is also the leader in the region when it comes to gender equality. The Government of the Republic of Serbia is led by a female prime minister and consists of almost 50 percent of women. The posts of heads of city and municipal administrations are held by over seventy women. In the judiciary, 56 percent of public prosecutors are women. In courts of general jurisdiction, there are 69 percent of women and in courts of special jurisdiction 76.3 percent.

ALEKSANDAR VUČIĆ
President of Serbia

As a public good, democracy must have an implicit principle of nonexclusion, where the progress of humanity must be shared in an equitable and sustainable manner by all of its members.

CARLOS VILA NOVA
President of São Tomé and Príncipe

Diversity is our greatest strength since it allows for creativity and innovation in a globalized context.

GUY PARMELIN
President of Switzerland

[Eric Williams, former prime minister of Trinidad and Tobago] stressed that, and I quote, "Democracy means more than the right to vote. It includes the recognition of the rights of others and the responsibility of the government to protect its citizens and the subordination of the right of any race to the overriding right of the human race."

KEITH ROWLEY
Prime Minister of Trinidad and Tobago

Liberal democracy is not synonymous with only giving rights to people to choose their representatives. Often a majority in parliament is seen to ignore the rights of the minorities.

LIONEL AINGIMEA
President of Nauru

We need to devise and implement measures that give people the crucial assurance that every one of them plays an important role in our democratic system and has the power to influence it.

ANDREJ BABIŠ
Prime Minister of the Czech Republic

Our experience showed us that elections are necessary but not sufficient to guarantee an open and inclusive democracy.... In an inclusive democracy, on the other hand, every and all votes must hold equal value.

AIYAZ SAYED-KHAIYUM
Acting Prime Minister of Fiji

We must bolster support for programs that promote equal rights and opportunities. We also need to build support programs for people of African descent, victims of violent crimes, immigrants, refugees, people with disabilities, the homeless, the elderly, and any other vulnerable group that is the victim of discrimination.

LUIS LACALLE POU
President of Uruguay

In order to fight the erosion of trust in democratic structures, innovative government is needed, which engages with society in an inclusive fashion.

KATRÍN JAKOBSDÓTTIR
Prime Minister of Iceland

The threats of cultural relativism, from an international perspective, or the disaffection with democratic institutions in our own countries, are real. And to combat them, we must ensure that our societies adopt a new social contract, working mainly along two fronts. First, fighting inequality and exclusion. . . . Secondly, we also need to strengthen the mechanisms of social dialogue, transparency, and accountability.

PEDRO SÁNCHEZ
President of Spain

In order to fight the erosion of trust in democratic structures, innovative government is needed, which engages with society in an inclusive fashion.

KATRÍN JAKOBSDÓTTIR
Prime Minister of Iceland

At the national level, I would like to see the approval of an amendment to the law of political parties which establishes the principle of gender equality.

CARLOS VILA NOVA
President of São Tomé and Príncipe

More equality means better democracies.

PEDRO SÁNCHEZ
President of Spain

Election Integrity

The Mexican writer Octávio Paz said, "A nation without free elections is a nation without a voice, without eyes, and without arms." How true are these simple words that portray one of the fundamental principles of democracy: the free and transparent electoral process to choose leaders.

CARLOS ALVARADO QUESADA
President of Costa Rica

Free and fair elections are the foundation of democracy and a critical component of political freedom. There can be no democracy without free and fair elections.

ANDREJ BABIŠ
Prime Minister of the Czech Republic

Out of duty toward our children and grandchildren,
we will not give up when it comes to deepening
our democracy, guaranteeing the integrity of the
electoral process, and consolidating peace through the
establishment of accurate electoral registers, the due
validation of candidatures, the material organization
of ballots, and the proclamations of authentic results.

NANA AKUFO-ADDO
President of Ghana

The very foundation of American democracy [is]
the sacred right of every person to make their voice
heard through free, fair, and secure elections.

JOSEPH R. BIDEN
President of the United States

We need more effective democracies. We
need elections with integrity that legitimize
the winners and provide the public with
confidence in their leaders and institutions.

MARCELO REBELO DE SOUSA
President of Portugal

The concept of free and fair elections is a fragile one which must be zealously guarded by those with power to govern and vigorously monitored by the governed.

TIMOTHY HARRIS
*Prime Minister of Saint Kitts
and Nevis*

Poland shall continue to be a promoter of democracy, because I believe that my daughter, born in 1995, who has not lived a second in a dictatorship, and her Belarusian peer, who has never seen free elections, are two equal people with equal rights.

ANDRZEJ DUDA
President of Poland

My administration will ensure an honest, peaceful, credible and free elections in May. It will be my highest honor to turn over the reins of power to my successor.

RODRIGO DUTERTE
President of the Philippines

Today representative democracy remains alive and well in Barbados, with free and fair elections as its bedrock.

MIA AMOR MOTTLEY
Prime Minister of Barbados

The strength of any democracy is very much determined by the credibility of its electoral process and respect for the will of the people.

NANA AKUFO-ADDO
President of Ghana

I am saying this not only as the president of the Republic of Poland. I am saying these words as Andrzej Duda, who in 2025 will end his presidency and hand over power to his democratically elected male or female successor. And then he will proudly become an ordinary citizen again, simply a voter.

ANDRZEJ DUDA
President of Poland

We believe that our peoples are entitled to elect and remove their governments through the ballot box, overseen by independent courts and a free media.

BORIS JOHNSON
Prime Minister of United Kingdom

The bedrock of a true democracy is securely grounded in the exercise of free and fair elections at specifically expressed, regular intervals.

TIMOTHY HARRIS
Prime Minister of Saint Kitts and Nevis

Rule of Law

A commitment to eschew authoritarian rule, adhere to
the separation of powers, maintain transparency and
an accountable electoral process are all imperatives
for a democracy tethered to the rule of law.

TIMOTHY HARRIS
Prime Minister of Saint Kitts and Nevis

The rule of law underpins our democracy by
guaranteeing that the government as well as
the people are accountable under the law.

CHANDRIKAPERSAD SANTOKHI
President of Suriname

Democracy is not only consolidated with fair and free elections to choose the leader who will serve and represent the people for a certain period. Men pass on, but institutions remain . . . which is why the effective implementation and enforcement of the constitution and other laws is absolutely necessary.

CARLOS VILA NOVA
President of São Tomé and Príncipe

Respect for the principles of democratic accountability, human rights, and the rule of law have enabled us to oversee eight presidential elections in the fourth republic, with five presidential transitions and three peaceful transfers of power through the ballot box, from one party to the other.

NANA AKUFO-ADDO
President of Ghana

The rule of law is one aspect which ensures that we know that the consequences of our actions are not arbitrary but are prescribed by laws.

CHANDRIKAPERSAD SANTOKHI
President of Suriname

The main lessons of our development as a society upholding the rule of law in the last three decades is that no achievement should be taken for granted.

RUMEN RADEV
President of Bulgaria

The rule of law applies to everyone, even those entrusted with official responsibilities by their peers in society.

CHANDRIKAPERSAD SANTOKHI
President of Suriname

The promotion of the rule of law also fundamentally requires a social contract among individuals, civil society, the media, the government, the police, and all other sectors of society to fight corruption.

CHANDRIKAPERSAD SANTOKHI
President of Suriname

Judicial Independence

Our judicial reforms are the bedrock of
our governance architecture, and we view
judicial independence as sacrosanct.

HAGE G. GEINGOB
President of Namibia

The court, of course, is one of the tripartite institutions,
along with the executive and the legislature, which
ensures separation of powers and prevents the
foundations of democracy from being eroded.

TIMOTHY HARRIS
Prime Minister of Saint Kitts and Nevis

Access to justice and respect for human rights go hand in hand. However, our political realities are that limitations on human rights are sometimes placed in the hands of the executive. An independent and fair judiciary with an appellate process provides an avenue for those aggrieved by executive decisions to a secure enforcement of those rights.

LIONEL AINGIMEA
President of Nauru

The judiciary . . . has become a critical element in our overall democratic transition. In the 1990s, we strengthened judiciary independence. . . . We are now finishing reforms to increase the judges' accountability while also improving their professional expertise and impartiality.

ZUZANA ČAPUTOVÁ
President of Slovakia

As a nation, Nauru believes in ensuring that every person has access to a free and fair justice system.

LIONEL AINGIMEA
President of Nauru

On the two occasions in which disputes have arisen over the results of elections, it was in the court, and not on the streets, that the matters were satisfactorily resolved.

NANA AKUFO-ADDO
President of Ghana

Free and Independent Media

A free and independent media is the bedrock of democracy. It is how publics stay informed and how governments are held accountable.

JOSEPH R. BIDEN
President of the United States

Free media is the lifeline of democracy.

KAJA KALLAS
Prime Minister of Estonia

Every healthy democracy needs journalists
who can independently investigate, report,
and hold governments to account.

MARK RUTTE
Prime Minister of the Netherlands

The freedom of speech in global platforms
should be guaranteed. Censorship, even if well
intended, contradicts democratic principles.

EGILS LEVITS
President of Latvia

More and more media freedom is being trampled
underfoot. Media outlets are being forced to close.
Journalists are being sued, threatened, and even
killed. We must stand firm and reverse this trend.

MARK RUTTE
Prime Minister of the Netherlands

Free and independent media, including the non-governmental sector, remain the basis for the development and survival of any democratic society.

ZDRAVKO KRIVOKAPIĆ
Prime Minister of Montenegro

I have unequivocally expressed the irrevocable commitment of the Namibian government to media freedom by stating that as long as I'm the president of the Namibian republic no journalist will be arrested or detained on the basis of their work.

HAGE G. GEINGOB
President of Namibia

A significant threat to Micronesia's democracy is our lack of free media. We have only one newspaper in our country, which has limited staff and no legal right to information from the government. This is unsustainable and must change.

DAVID W. PANUELO
President of Micronesia

Two of the most important defenses against the fall into a spiral toward dictatorship are the free press and independent electoral organs.

SEBASTIÁN PIÑERA
President of Chile

Freedom of speech and media freedom is a crucial component of democracy. However, equally important is unbiased reporting by journalists themselves, which is unfortunately being replaced by activists and the pushing of certain agendas.

ANDREJ BABIŠ
Prime Minister of the Czech Republic

Any democracy needs free and independent media.

ALEXANDER SCHALLENBERG
Former Chancellor of Austria

Truth, Transparency, and Trust

Democracy relies on trust. Trust is built on fairness, accountability, transparency, and the rule of law. This Summit for Democracy is a moment to show that democracies, above all other models, are rising to today's challenges and delivering for our people.

CHARLES MICHEL
President of the European Council

I believe in democracy with the understanding that it is a collective human right that represents society, and it serves justice and truth.

MARIO ABDO BENÍTEZ
President of Paraguay

Democracy is the conversation and
mutual understanding between us.

METTE FREDERIKSEN
Prime Minister of Denmark

The more transparent and accountable we are,
the healthier our democracy is altogether.

NAFTALI BENNETT
Prime Minister of Israel

Romania is determined to prevent and combat all
negative phenomena undermining democratic trust,
thus contributing to building democratic resilience.

KLAUS IOHANNIS
President of Romania

Our governments are elected by the people, and in
doing so, they bestow their trust in their leaders.

LIONEL AINGIMEA
President of Nauru

The power of democracy emanates from
people's trust in transparency and fairness.

MOON JAE-IN
President of the Republic of Korea

Do not underestimate the need for trust
between citizens and their representatives.

JONAS GAHR STØRE
Prime Minister of Norway

Today Bulgaria stands firm on its democratic path.
And we shall focus our future efforts on the effective
prosecution of corruption, on building accountable
administration, on safeguarding media freedom, and
on promoting the citizens' trust in institutions. The
latter shall be the ultimate indicator of our success.

RUMEN RADEV
President of Bulgaria

We are convinced that the best defense for
democracy is a citizenry whose demands are met
by an honest, efficient, and transparent state.

PEDRO CASTILLO
President of Peru

Differences in political and ideological views are,
in my opinion, not a problem. The problem is
unwillingness to engage in dialogue—a dialogue
which means not only presentation of one's own
views but also a willingness to reconcile views.

BORUT PAHOR
President of Slovenia

"To give no trust is to get no trust." As democracies,
we must trust our citizens and invest in public
infrastructure in the digital realm. This is the best and
only way to protect and advance our shared values.

AUDREY TANG
Digital Minister of Taiwan

Democracy is transparency,
commitment, and accountability.

MARIO ABDO BENÍTEZ
President of Paraguay

Accountability and transparency guard against
corruption and financial misconduct in public office.

TIMOTHY HARRIS
Prime Minister of Saint Kitts and Nevis

We intend to introduce legislative transparency by
making all votes public so that constituents can hold
their lawmakers accountable for their actions, which
is a fundamental element of any healthy democracy.

GEORGE WEAH
President of Liberia

We are very much aware in Ghana that if we seek to
prolong our democratic journey we need to enhance
transparency and accountability in our governance

structures and build strong institutions that can fight corruption and the wanton dissipation of public funds.

NANA AKUFO-ADDO
President of Ghana

The strongest democracies ensure their citizens know what their government is doing, how they are governing, and why they are governing the way they are.

DAVID W. PANUELO
President of Micronesia

Economic Justice

Hunger and want know not democracy.

JOHN BRICEÑO
Prime Minister of Belize

We have to move from an electoral democracy to
an effective democracy that guarantees the rights to
health, education, drinking water, equal opportunity,
housing, employment, and dignified treatment.

PEDRO CASTILLO
President of Peru

We are devoted to the ambition of empowering prosperity for every citizen of our country, and to achieving this within a framework of democracy.

MOHAMED IRFAAN ALI
President of Guyana

Democracy must address people's livelihoods and their desires for a better life.

SHER BAHADUR DEUBA
Prime Minister of Nepal

It is necessary to address the economic aspect— that is, to prevent the division between the rich and the poor and to protect the middle class, who are at the heart of a robust democracy.

KISHIDA FUMIO
Prime Minister of Japan

Only by creating a more just and equitable society will we really ensure that our democracy delivers for the needs of our people.

HAGE G. GEINGOB
President of Namibia

At the end of the day, democracy must bring
prosperity and welfare to the people.

JOKO WIDODO
President of Indonesia

We have the obligation to adopt policies with
a real impact on people's daily livelihoods, on
their salaries, on their access to housing, on
universal and quality health and education.

PEDRO SÁNCHEZ
President of Spain

Global inequity and practices which perpetuate poverty,
unemployment, and crime have contributed to weaken
democracies and to collapse of many of them.

GASTON BROWNE
Prime Minister of Antigua and Barbuda

At its most basic, a democracy that works for the
people is one rooted in the economic certainty
and financial security of the progressive center
ground, not in the extremes of Left and the Right.

KYRIAKOS MITSOTAKIS
Prime Minister of Greece

Democracy, my friends, must be rooted in the elimination of poverty and the assurance of freedoms. And, fundamentally, freedom is about one's right to choose, and hence it is inextricably linked to the elimination of poverty.

MIA AMOR MOTTLEY
Prime Minister of Barbados

True democratic freedom is impossible to sustain in the absence of economic equity.

HAGE G. GEINGOB
President of Namibia

For many of our countries that are fully committed to democracy, people empowerment—feeding the hungry, housing the displaced, and providing jobs to the unemployed—are the biggest challenges to democracy.

GASTON BROWNE
Prime Minister of Antigua and Barbuda

A people deprived of an economic or social existence will have no appetite for democratic ideals.

MIA AMOR MOTTLEY
Prime Minister of Barbados

The challenge of our times is to protect and consolidate democracy in this complex, multidimensional global scenario, to guarantee the dignity of the people through the eradication of extreme poverty in the creation of opportunities, and to ensure the right to a habitable planet earth through climate action.

ULISSES CORREIA E SILVA
Prime Minister of Cabo Verde

Democracy is not sustainable without economic and social development, to which human and political rights are essential but not sufficient.

GASTON BROWNE
Prime Minister of Antigua and Barbuda

To flourish, people must have the democratic system work for them. They must see the principles of democracy in action in their day-to-day lives in ways that improve their socioeconomic standing.

AIYAZ SAYED-KHAIYUM
Acting Prime Minister of Fiji

The widening gap between the rich and the poor
is one of the factors that most affects political
stability and weakens our democracies.

PEDRO SÁNCHEZ
President of Spain

There can be no true democracy without
the development of our people.

MIA AMOR MOTTLEY
Prime Minister of Barbados

The threats to democracy have many guises,
from drowning out the voice of the people, to
the denial of opportunity, to the erection of
barriers of social and economic inequity.

ROOSEVELT SKERRIT
Prime Minister of Dominica

Widening disparities and worsening inequalities, caused
by free competition, is hampering social unity and
endangering democracy. As we face serious challenges—
infectious diseases, the climate crisis, globalization and
social polarization—it is time for us to mull over how
to defend and advance democracy and find solutions.

MOON JAE-IN
President of the Republic of Korea

Democracy must not be divorced from development. In the global community, each is dependent on the other. This summit must recognize that truth and act on it.

MOHAMED IRFAAN ALI

President of Guyana

Climate Justice

Our democracies will not survive without climate justice.

JOHN BRICEÑO
Prime Minister of Belize

The poor, the unemployed, the hungry, and those
who are being displaced from their homelands
as result of climate change caused by others will
not long remain peaceful and law-abiding. And
political opportunists will take advantage of these
conditions for narrow partisan gain, as you have
seen occur in even the greatest democracies.

GASTON BROWNE
Prime Minister of Antigua and Barbuda

One of today's central missions is reversing the causes of climate change and environmental pollution, which are leading humanity toward a possible disaster.

GUILLERMO LASSO
President of Ecuador

The biggest challenge we collectively face in the longer term is the climate crisis.

KATRÍN JAKOBSDÓTTIR
Prime Minister of Iceland

If the green transition increases inequality, we can be sure of one thing: we will not succeed.

JONAS GAHR STØRE
Prime Minister of Norway

At this historic juncture, democracy, peace, and environmental conservation are the essential pillars needed to drive the world's economies and policies.

GUILLERMO LASSO
President of Ecuador

If we are to navigate the challenges of our time,
including COVID-19 and climate change, we will need
to do so in a way that reflects our key strengths—
the inclusivity of our societies, which allow us to
acknowledge and value a diversity of voices—
and build enduring institutions and approaches
to help solve challenges and address needs.

JACINDA ARDERN
Prime Minister of New Zealand

The years ahead will be defined by the transition
to the low-emission economy in all countries.
That is the single most important task we're up
against and a stress test for our political systems.

JONAS GAHR STØRE
Prime Minister of Norway

For a small nation like Nauru, issues impacting the
environment are directly related to the livelihood
and survival of our people. We urge upon developed
countries to ensure that the Paris Agreement on
Climate Change be strengthened to ensure that the

bigger and economically powerful countries mitigate the losses suffered by countries such Nauru.

LIONEL AINGIMEA

President of Nauru

Civic Virtue

Democracy is not only about functioning democratic institutions. Democracy is also about very high levels of political and legal culture.

BORUT PAHOR
President of Slovenia

Perhaps it was best said by Pericles, the preeminent statesman of classical Athens, the cradle of democracy, who said, "What you leave behind is not what is engraved in stone monuments, but what is woven into the lives of others."

NICOS ANASTASIADES
President of Cyprus

Mindful that democracy is a process that must be nurtured, we are implementing good governance standards across all spheres of government.

MUHAMMADU BUHARI
President of Nigeria

The structural features, like multiparty elections, independent judiciary, and free media, are important instruments of democracy. However, the basic strength of democracy is the spirit and ethos that lie within our citizens and our societies. Democracy is not only of the people, by the people, for the people but also with the people, within the people.

NARENDRA MODI
Prime Minister of India

Democracy must be lived and felt by each and every citizen.

MARCELO REBELO DE SOUSA
President of Portugal

What is the heart of our democracy? Is it our laws? Our political system? Our institutions? More than

Seventy years ago, the Danish writer Hal Koch
answered this question. Democracy, he argued, is
not just a system of government. It is a way of life.

METTE FREDERIKSEN
Prime Minister of Denmark

If we want democracy to prevail, we must
choose the path of decency and strength.

NAFTALI BENNETT
Prime Minister of Israel

We must also work domestically to demand
diligence, engagement, and accountability
from our citizens and leaders.

SURANGEL S. WHIPPS JR.
President of Palau

The democratic community in Bulgaria relies
deeply on the professionalism of the European
public prosecutor's office investigating the
corruption and fraud with EU funds.

RUMEN RADEV
President of Bulgaria

Global Unity

The destiny of our democracies depends on each other.

URSULA VON DER LEYEN
President of the European Commission

Let us join hands for a better, more peaceful,
prosperous, and more democratic world.

HAKAINDE HICHILEMA
President of Zambia

Let us work together to make democracy
the best guarantor of world peace.

ALBERTO FERNÁNDEZ
President of Argentina

If we are to restore the appeal of democracy throughout the world, we need to join forces to face these challenges together.

NIKOL PASHINYAN
Prime Minister of Armenia

We must work together to bolster and defend our democracies, as like-minders aligning together with unity and purpose.

SCOTT MORRISON
Prime Minister of Australia

Let us work continuously to deliver on the rich promise of democracy—that all citizens can live in peace with dignity and are afforded equal opportunities to fulfill their destiny.

JOHN BRICEÑO
Prime Minister of Belize

From engagements with civil society, to reforms to strengthen democratic institutions,

we have an immense opportunity today to
learn from each other's experiences.

ANTONY BLINKEN
US Secretary of State

Small countries cannot meet these challenges
alone. Other large and richer states must help meet
these challenges, or it will not be long before the
deleterious effects end up on the shores of the rich,
shaking the foundations of democracy globally.

GASTON BROWNE
Prime Minister of Antigua and Barbuda

The defense of democracy needs all of us.

ALEXANDER SCHALLENBERG
Former Chancellor of Austria

Inaction is not an option.

JOSEPH R. BIDEN
President of the United States

Collaboration and cooperation among democracies will lead to new reforms and measures that will meet emergent challenges.

JOHN BRICEÑO
Prime Minister of Belize

A question which remains, however, is whether countries can be successful in their struggle for democracy if they stand alone.

RUMEN RADEV
President of Bulgaria

While democracy starts at home, building a safer and more prosperous world depends on all of us working together.

JUSTIN TRUDEAU
Prime Minister of Canada

The dynamics of the global power relations demands more than ever our united response. The fundamental values we stand for are more than a point of ethics or identity. They serve as a navigating tool in the face of rapid changes in global trends as well as the anchor and the safe harbor during geopolitical crisis.

ANDREJ PLENKOVIĆ
Prime Minister of Croatia

Democratic enhancement and renewal, therefore, require global effort; one that takes full account of the multidimensional aspects of democracy, including the provision of conditions for economic progress.

MOHAMED IRFAAN ALI
President of Guyana

We must work together as an international community, defending democracy and freedoms as we preserve peace and join efforts to ensure the best possible future for our peoples.

GUILLERMO LASSO
President of Ecuador

Let us support one another and use our combined influence to bolster our democracies. I hope we will make 2022 a year of joint action and wish us all the success in accomplishing it.

KAJA KALLAS
Prime Minister of Estonia

The global chain of freedom is only as strong as its weakest link.

MOHAMED IRFAAN ALI
President of Guyana

Grenada acknowledges the interdependent nature
of our world and the fundamental importance
of maintaining hemispheric stability, and
ensuring that our Caribbean region remains a
zone of peace and bastion for democracy.

KEITH C. MITCHELL
Prime Minister of Grenada

Democracy cannot be maintained nationally
unless it is sustained internationally.

MOHAMED IRFAAN ALI
President of Guyana

By working together, democracies can meet
the aspirations of our citizens and celebrate the
democratic spirit of humanity. India stands ready
to join fellow democracies in this noble endeavor.

NARENDRA MODI
Prime Minister of India

We need to be consistent. Democracy must be
promoted beyond our national borders. Democracy
must also feature in the conduct between nations.

JOKO WIDODO
President of Indonesia

It's up to the international community to take action
and commit to a more democratic and moral world.

NAFTALI BENNETT
Prime Minister of Israel

It was only the vigilance of the Guyanese people,
supported by a watchful international community,
that prevented Guyana from being plunged into a
dictatorship with all its disastrous consequences.

MOHAMED IRFAAN ALI
President of Guyana

No democracy is safe unless all
democracies are protected.

KEITH C. MITCHELL
Prime Minister of Grenada

I hope the summit can be our reminder to
strengthen democracy at the global level in order
to avoid the "mighty takes all" situation.

JOKO WIDODO
President of Indonesia

It is up to us as a global community to stand
up to corruption, to fight against tyranny,
and to choose right over wrong.

NAFTALI BENNETT
Prime Minister of Israel

In order to make democracy take root in a country,
it is important to stand and work with that country.

KISHIDA FUMIO
Prime Minister of Japan

As inequality and inequities are revealed and deepened
by the pandemic, as people demand more from
constrained governments, the global community
of democratic nations needs to actively promote
a multilateral system that fosters fairness in trade,
protects the planet, and guarantees the security
and human rights of the people of the world.

ANDREW HOLNESS
Prime Minister of Jamaica

A rules-based international order is fundamental
to the sustainability of democracies.

EGILS LEVITS
President of Latvia

We must come together, work together, and shine
the light of freedom, liberty, and democracy.

NAFTALI BENNETT
Prime Minister of Israel

We look forward to working with our partners
as we seek to learn from each other, to share
and exchange experiences, and to commit to
strengthening our democracy and promoting
democratic principles and ideals globally.

ANDREW HOLNESS
Prime Minister of Jamaica

Democracies should be more visible globally
and display responsible leadership.

EGILS LEVITS
President of Latvia

In order to achieve our goals, we must all work
together. Democracy must not only be protected
internally but also promoted externally.

XAVIER BETTEL
President of Luxembourg

The pandemic has taught us that success can be achieved through concerted and consolidated efforts by all global stakeholders. To ensure strong democracies, to ensure human rights, we need to replicate the same effort.

IBRAHIM MOHAMED SOLI
President of Maldives

Strengthening democracy across the world is indeed a noble ambition—the greatest gift we, as leaders, can give to our citizens, both present and future.

ROBERT ABELA
Prime Minister of Malta

Democracy and promotion of human rights cannot exist in a vacuum. The respect of the international rule of law, as well as the promotion of a rules-based system where the sovereignty and territorial integrity of every country is respected, represent crucial components of global governance.

PRAVIND KUMAR JUGNAUTH
Prime Minister of Mauritius

Let us use the opportunity presented by this summit
to renew our collective and individual commitments
to our more equal democratic global society.

ESTEBAN MOCTEZUMA
Ambassador of Mexico

Micronesia encourages our first and foremost ally, the
United States of America, to consider the passage of the
John R. Lewis Voting Rights Advancement Act of 2021,
as Micronesia's own national security relies on American
democracy thriving as a beacon for the world to follow.

DAVID W. PANUELO
President of Micronesia

Our alliances have helped us reinforce our
sovereignty and withstand those who wish to
undermine and corrupt or democratic institutions.

SURANGEL S. WHIPPS JR.
President of Palau

Considering the magnitude of crises that slow
down these efforts today, not only in Moldova
but in all young and fragile democracies across

the globe, there is an urgent need for global solidarity and leadership to protect democracy.

MAIA SANDU
President of Moldova

Our actions today in strengthening the international rules-based order is democracy's prosperity tomorrow.

DAVID W. PANUELO
President of Micronesia

We must harness the forces of our countries in a global alliance to advance human rights worldwide to ensure that democracy persists.

SURANGEL S. WHIPPS JR.
President of Palau

We need to believe more than ever in the good forces of multilateralism, cooperation, and global solidarity. Togetherness in times of crisis is our best shield—our best chance at saving democracy.

MAIA SANDU
President of Moldova

Namibia stands ready to hold hands with all the world's democracies to strengthen democracy and pull in one direction: toward an inclusive, stable, peaceful and prosperous future built on respect for human rights and economic aspirations of all the citizens.

HAGE G. GEINGOB
President of Namibia

Democratic states, we must unite and lead the charge to help liberate oppressed societies.

SURANGEL S. WHIPPS JR.
President of Palau

It is our duty to uphold the democratic values and principles we all cherish. It is also vital to coordinate at the global level.

KLAUS IOHANNIS
President of Romania

We have achieved fundamental progress building our own democratic institutions and are a reliable partner for all who today are ready to come to the defense of democracy and freedom in the

world. By coming together, we will make the
world freer, safer, and more democratic.

VOLODYMYR ZELENSKY
President of Ukraine

We urge the international community to play
an ever bolder role in supporting democracy,
amplifying and empowering the voices of the
marginalized, both across Africa and the world.

HAKAINDE HICHILEMA
President of Zambia

We need a set of global rules when
it comes to disinformation.

METTE FREDERIKSEN
Prime Minister of Denmark

We have to take collective action for the sake of
human rights and for the sake of doing what is right.

NAFTALI BENNETT
Prime Minister of Israel

As democracies, we have a duty to each other and to the world. We must live up to our commitment to freedom, fairness, and economic prosperity for all.

MARIO DRAGHI
Prime Minister of Italy

For countries like mine, the Republic of Moldova, which has been struggling for three decades to overcome the perils of a prolonged democratic transition, strengthening democracy means everything today.

MAIA SANDU
President of Moldova

It is essential that democracy not only survive but prosper. In this regard, Micronesia solicits fellow democracies to review our democratic process, as it is imperative that elections be free, fair, and accessible.

DAVID W. PANUELO
President of Micronesia

Only when political will at home to undertake the most difficult reforms is backed up by international support can democracy face and overcome the force of disinformation, populism, crumbling institutions, rising inequalities, and conflicts.

MAIA SANDU
President of Moldova

The world's democracies, with all our flaws and challenges, must show that democracy can deliver—to improve people's lives and to tackle the biggest global challenges we face.

URSULA VON DER LEYEN
President of the European Commission

As always, the strongest power we have in overcoming crises is our collective intelligence—democracy.

MOON JAE-IN
President of the Republic of Korea

Acknowledgments

I owe a debt of gratitude to many people for helping to bring *How to Save Democracy* to fruition. Among them, I want especially to thank David Brodwin, friend and executive fellow at the Center for Higher Ambition Leadership, who read the first iteration of the book and recommended numerous improvements, including dramatic changes to the title and subtitle; Tom Comitta, talented artist and bibliophile who partnered with me in the original design and organization of the book; Harrison Hobart, friend and sharp-minded critic of my writing and daily booster of my efforts to get *American Commonwealth* off the ground; Nick Zeppos, Jeff Balser, Keith Meador, Marshall Eakin, and Stephan Heckers, all leaders at Vanderbilt who gave me an intellectual home as a visiting scholar as I transitioned from doctoring to full-time writing and advocacy on behalf of ethical constitutional democracy; John Geer and Alan Wiseman for inviting me to join the Vanderbilt Department of Political Science; Naren Aryal, Jenna Scafuri, and the rest of the excellent production team at Amplify Publishing; Jenn Hanson-dePaula, book publicist and everyday enthusiast of *How to Save Democracy*; Natasha Lasky, editor and writer who offered critical feedback on the introduction, title, and subtitle; and, not least, Josh Graham Lynn and Ross Sherman at RepresentUs for partnering in the book's mission to strengthen democracy through active citizenship and ethical leadership.

For their input and support, I would also like to thank numerous other friends, colleagues, and commenters on *American Commonwealth*, including Gretchen Sisson, Deb Daugherty, Robert Harris, Marsha Vande Berg, Matthew Finlay, Amy Atkinson, Mark Atkinson, Casey Botticello, Ted Fischer, Bruce Linenberg, Cathryn Lewis, Tim Cermak, Angus Parker, Keel Hunt, Ira Glick, Kelly Eden, Anthony Williams, Wendi Gordon, Edward Alvarez, Vanessa Burnett, Andrew McAllister, Peter Fry, Paul Fishman, Hal Candee, Eliza Brown, Mark Dykeman, John Pinto, Blyth Lord, John Englander, Heather Corcoran, and Jay O'Connor, among others.

Finally, I wish to thank family members Rosana Castrillo Díaz, Alejandro Merritt, Cameron Merritt, Louise Merritt, Stroud Merritt, Gilbert Merritt, and Fields Livingston for their support and encouragement. Especially my father, Gilbert Merritt, lifelong defender of democracy, who passed down to me the "spirit of liberty"—as he recited so often from a speech by Judge Learned Hand in 1944—without which this book never would have been conceived or achieved.

About

Eli Merritt is a historian at Vanderbilt University who has written political commentary for the *New York Times*, *Los Angeles Times*, *Seattle Times*, *USA Today*, *Chicago Tribune*, and *Philadelphia Inquirer*, among other news outlets. He writes a newsletter called *American Commonwealth* that explores the origins of the United States' political discontents and solutions to them. Trained in history, ethics, medicine, and psychiatry, he has served on medical ethics committees at Vanderbilt and Stanford. His academic specialties are ethical leadership in democracy, the intersection of demagogues and democracy, and the politics of the founding era of the United States. He is the editor of *The Curse of Demagogues: Lessons Learned from the Presidency of Donald J. Trump* and the author of *Disunion Among Ourselves: The Perilous Politics of the American Revolution*. Find Eli online at elimerritt.com and elimerritt.substack.com.

Joshua Graham Lynn, cofounder and CEO of RepresentUs, has dedicated his career to mobilizing millions of Americans toward a better future. A seasoned storyteller, communications specialist, and creative director, his work has been honored by the Rebrand 100 Awards, the Webby Awards, the American Package Design Awards, and the ADDYs. Josh has launched and managed numerous international brands and developed power-building platforms for organizations ranging from credit unions to sustainable communities.

RepresentUs is one of America's leading nonpartisan organizations building a movement to fight corruption and make government more accountable to the people. Founded in 2012, RepresentUs and the anti-corruption movement have won more than 170 state and local victories to give voters more power, representation, and confidence in democracy. Each victory, from Ranked Choice Voting to campaign finance reform, or Vote by Mail to anti-gerrymandering laws, brings us one step closer to making America the world's strongest democracy. Find Josh and RepresentUs online at Represent.Us, Facebook (@RepresentUs), and Twitter (@representus).